THE NEAT METHOD
ORGANIZING
RECIPE BOOK

THE NEAT METHOD

ORGANIZING

RECIPE BOOK

70 Simple Projects to Take Your Home from Chaos to Composed

Ashley Murphy & Marissa Hagmeyer

ARTISAN | NEW YORK

To our children—Ben, Will, Hazel, and Isla—who have taught us to be curious, to be fearless, and, most important, to love deeply!

Library of Congress Cataloging-in-Publication Data is on file.

ISBN 978-1-64829-354-2

Design by Nina Simoneaux

Artisan books may be purchased in bulk for business, educational, or promotional use. For information, please contact your local bookseller or the Hachette Book Group Special Markets Department at special.markets@hbgusa.com.

The publisher is not responsible for websites (or their content) that are not owned by the publisher.

The Hachette Speakers Bureau provides a wide range of authors for speaking events. To find out more, go to hachettespeakersbureau.com or email HachetteSpeakers@hbgusa.com.

Published by Artisan,
an imprint of Workman Publishing,
a division of Hachette Book Group, Inc.
1290 Avenue of the Americas
New York, NY 10104
artisanbooks.com

The Artisan name and logo are registered trademarks of Hachette Book Group, Inc.

Printed in China on responsibly sourced paper
First printing, November 2024

10 9 8 7 6 5 4 3 2 1

CONTENTS

Introduction   9

Getting Started   13

Kitchen & Pantry   25

Bedroom   57

Bathroom & Linen Closet   87

Kids' Spaces   109

Laundry   135

Storage & Utility Spaces   145

Entryway   173

Garage   185

The 7-Day Reset   201

Acknowledgments   204

Index   205

Introduction

When it comes to caring for their homes, some people claim to possess the elusive "organizing gene," while others deny its existence in their genetic code. But here's a secret we've uncovered as two women who are so passionate about organization we've made it our livelihoods: having that gene isn't a prerequisite for living an organized life. Through our business, NEAT Method, we've helped many people create homes that work for them regardless of their inherent organizational skills.

That said, we definitely have the gene. Our childhoods in the Midwest may have seemed ordinary, but our affection for tidiness was anything but. We both found ourselves rearranging our rooms incessantly, creating household rules that our siblings and friends couldn't escape, and living by the mantra of coloring inside the lines. This shared love of organization and a desire to make a difference in the lives of others became the driving force behind what we came to call NEAT Method.

In the beginning, our mission was simply to transform clients' spaces from chaotic to composed. We discovered that once their homes were in order, our clients experienced more than just physical transformations: their moods lifted, their motivation surged, and their days flowed with newfound efficiency. Home organization was no longer just a business venture; it was a calling.

We knew that to magnify our impact, we had to expand our reach. This led us to search for kindred spirits who shared our values and mission, offering franchise opportunities to others looking to turn their passion for home organization into a career. It was a bold leap, but after over a decade of growth, we're proud to say that we not only found the right individuals (and are still finding them) but also made a far more profound impact than we could have ever imagined. Each year, thousands of spaces—and lives—are transformed, thanks to all of our incredible clients trusting us within their homes.

If someone had told us in the beginning that our humble side hustle would evolve into the multifaceted business it is today, we never would have believed them. But here we are, armed with an arsenal of tips and tricks for achieving an organized home.

Our ultimate goal: to inspire change, one space at a time. In this book, we'll break down NEAT Method's approach to organizing various areas in your home. Although the process may seem daunting, rest assured that we'll be your guides as you take small, manageable steps toward a more efficient and calmer living environment. Embrace whatever prompted you to open this book, and celebrate the accomplishments it empowers you to achieve, whether you reorganize a single drawer or your entire home!

The images throughout these pages illustrate our method. It is essential to the NEAT philosophy that organization be an extension of your home's design. Your aesthetic should flow from your walls into your closets and cabinets and through all of your living areas. Beautiful spaces are functional spaces. We believe that your home should be a sanctuary—a place of serenity where you can find peace after a long day's work. We hope you fall in love with your home as you embark on this journey toward living the NEAT life!

Remember to give yourself grace along the way, and trust that you can do this, even if you weren't born with the organizing gene. And please share your incredible transformations with us; you're not just a reader, you're now a cherished member of our community!

Getting Started

If you're anything like our clients, you're filled with excitement about organizing your home yet uncertain of how and where to begin. We encourage you to pause, take a deep breath, and release any apprehension! Fear has no place in this process, and our commitment is to transform organizing from an intimidating chore into a fun and manageable endeavor.

Being organized is a habit, and as when building any new habit, the key is to begin with baby steps. Successfully completing small projects can provide you with those quick victories that serve as fuel to get you to the next phase. The "recipes" within this book include an indication of how long they will take to execute, from just a few minutes to a full day. There are many bite-sized projects that you can tackle one at a time, gradually transforming entire rooms in your home. The perfect place to start is the one drawer or cabinet that you most dread opening each day. Each recipe you complete will not only enhance your living environment but also sharpen your efficiency and proficiency in the art of home organization.

Before diving in, take a moment to review our method and the recommended tool kit detailed in the following pages. We wholeheartedly advocate preparation, and these sections will equip you with everything you need for success.

Ready to get started? You've got this!

The NEAT Method

As you progress through the projects, you might begin to think that we repeat ourselves—a lot. You're right! We do. Our method is a straight-forward six-step process that, once mastered, can be used to success-fully organize any corner of any room in your home.

1. SORT AND CATEGORIZE

The first step in any organizing project is to create an even bigger mess than the one you're trying to fix. Remove everything—we mean E-V-E-R-Y-T-H-I-N-G—from the cabinet, shelf, or drawer (or what-ever area you're tackling). Now that you have some breathing room, give the space a quick wipe-down or vacuum. Then sort everything you've removed into categories. At this point, there's no need to make decisions beyond grouping like with like. You might be shocked when you see what you have.

2. EDIT

This is the make-or-break step. (We like to call it "editing" instead of decluttering or purging to use a gentler term for a process that can be difficult.) Start with the low-hanging fruit: a category that isn't beloved or doesn't have an emotional tie. It will be easier to get into the rhythm by starting with socks rather than your vintage tee collection.

If you question whether you should get rid of something, create a "maybe" pile. Place those items in a box and store it out of the way in a closet, basement, or garage. If after one month you haven't reached for it, donate the items without a second look.

During this step, you'll also want to create "Relocate," "Mend," and "Give Away/Recycle/Toss" bags. We like to use grocery bags or the free reusable bags that tend to pile up around a home.

3. DECIDE WHAT GOES WHERE

The foundation of an organizing system is zones: designated spaces in each room for categories of items that are used at the same time or in a similar fashion. For zones to be effective, they need to contain everything pertinent to the activities taking place in them and be located near a compatible zone. Compatible zones in a kitchen, for example, would be a cabinet for everyday dishware and a dishwasher.

In addition to these zones, you'll want to identify the prime real estate in each room: the shelf, cabinet, or drawer that's easiest to access. This should be reserved for your most-used items. For example, your everyday watch should be stored at eye level. If it's not easy to find and put away, you'll never use it, or if you do, you'll never put it away where it belongs. How often you use the items in a zone dictates how far it should be placed from your room's prime real estate.

Finally, don't be afraid to think outside the box when deciding where to place organizing systems in your home. The entire purpose of this endeavor is to make daily activities quicker and easier to accomplish. If you prefer to brush your teeth after eating breakfast, consider keeping your toothbrush and toothpaste in the powder room next to your kitchen so you can brush and head straight out the door. Maybe you'll want to store kids' pajamas in a bathroom drawer for a smoother transition from bath time to bedtime.

4. ADD ORGANIZATIONAL PRODUCTS

Once you have all of your categories in place, it's time to add boundaries in the form of organizational products. This step establishes a system you can maintain while extending the beauty of your home to the organization spaces within it. Our philosophy is to select multifunctional products that enhance your current design. We generally advise against highly specialized products. Typically, all you need is some sort of bin, drawer divider, turntable, and/or canister. This way, if you decide to change up your system or move, the products you've invested in can move to another room or to a new home.

A word of warning: too many sizes can diminish the visual impact of coordinating containers. We like to limit a space to two sizes. And when selecting containers for decanting (more on this on page 19), purchase those with dimensions that will accommodate the contents in the size you typically buy (this will help you avoid having to create "backstock" bins).

While product implementation is a necessary step for maintaining organization long-term, you can absolutely follow our method without investing in new items during this part of the process. There's nothing wrong with using what you have when you're starting out. That said, in the long run, using uniform containers does make a discernible difference. Matching bins with complementary products enhances not only your organization but also the overall look and feel of your home. When cabinets, closets, and drawers are well styled, it encourages everyone in the home to maintain the system.

Note: For simplicity's sake throughout the book, we are referring to both bins and baskets as "bins." In everyday organizing, though, we consider solid-sided containers "bins" and containers with open-weave sides "baskets."

A NOTE ON MEASURING

We love systems so much that we even suggest one for measuring! We like to record measurements as back (from front edge to back edge), across (from left to right when facing the shelf or drawer), and up (from bottom to top). When you are deciding which products to use, this system will help eliminate confusion about how they will fit in the space.

Always remember to take *internal* measurements. External measurements can be off by enough to affect the containers that you're planning to use. Drawer-pull screws and cabinet hinges are specific examples of items that can affect internal measurements. If you're measuring the length of a drawer or cabinet, hold the tape measure at the edge of any protruding hardware like screws or hinges. It's also important to note that some spaces, especially those under sinks, may have additional dimensions to consider due to plumbing, such as side heights or clearances.

5. PUT IT ALL TOGETHER

Once you have chosen your organizational products, it's time to fill them! For many categories, this will entail simply stashing items in their dedicated bin or canister. For others, you may want to consider decanting. Decanting household items can seem like a waste of time and money, but we believe it is the opposite. It can help prevent over-buying and simplify the act of making a shopping list. If you can see what you have, you won't just buy based on what you *think* you need. Conversely, an opaque cardboard cereal box can easily obscure a lack of cereal for tomorrow's breakfast (or tonight's midnight snack). If you can see that the cereal container is empty with a quick glance, you know it's time to pick up a new box.

Next comes the question of whether or not to label. There's the belt-and-suspenders approach of labeling everything, everywhere, all the time. There's also the more relaxed approach of labeling only when necessary to avoid confusion (e.g., for opaque containers or items that are easily confused, like flour and pancake mix). Do what feels right for your home and the people who live in it. When labeling, you want to hit that sweet spot between being too general and too specific. If your labels are too general, they won't guide people to the correct item, but if they are overly specific, that can create a restrictive system that overwhelms household members and can cause people to freeze with indecision.

Whichever way you decide to label, keep it consistent: use the same materials, font, type size, and naming conventions for all labels across your home. We highly recommend forgoing the handwritten route unless someone who lives in the home has impeccable handwriting. Otherwise, stick to printed labels or use a label maker.

Pro Tip

If you're going to use an electronic labeler, use Helvetica for the font. It is widely available and highly readable (even in smaller sizes), and its neutral design makes it appropriate for most interior design schemes.

6. MAINTAIN

When you first finish organizing a space, it will be Pinterest-perfect. Over time, the system should still work for you, but the area will become lived-in. And that's okay. The point of organization isn't to always have a pristine, photo-ready home. It's to be able to easily locate an item when you need it.

Like exercise or cleaning, being organized is not a one-and-done proposition (as much as we wish it were). Kids grow up, new hobbies are adopted, life happens, and everything needs to be reorganized accordingly. Rather than waiting to do a larger reset, many people like to do a quick touch-up at the end of the day or the beginning of the week. Focusing on high-traffic areas like kitchens, drop zones, and entrances for a few minutes a day can make all the difference. And don't feel discouraged if you find yourself needing to do some maintenance after the holidays, hosting houseguests, or a particularly busy workweek. That's normal. If you have a solid system in place, you should be able to get things back in order pretty quickly.

There's a problem, however, if your system needs constant upkeep. This typically means your system is overly rigid and too difficult to maintain. If this is happening, take a hard look at your space and determine if you either have too much stuff for each category or your categories are too specific (e.g., "Chips" rather than "Salty Snacks" or "Oatmeal" versus "Breakfast").

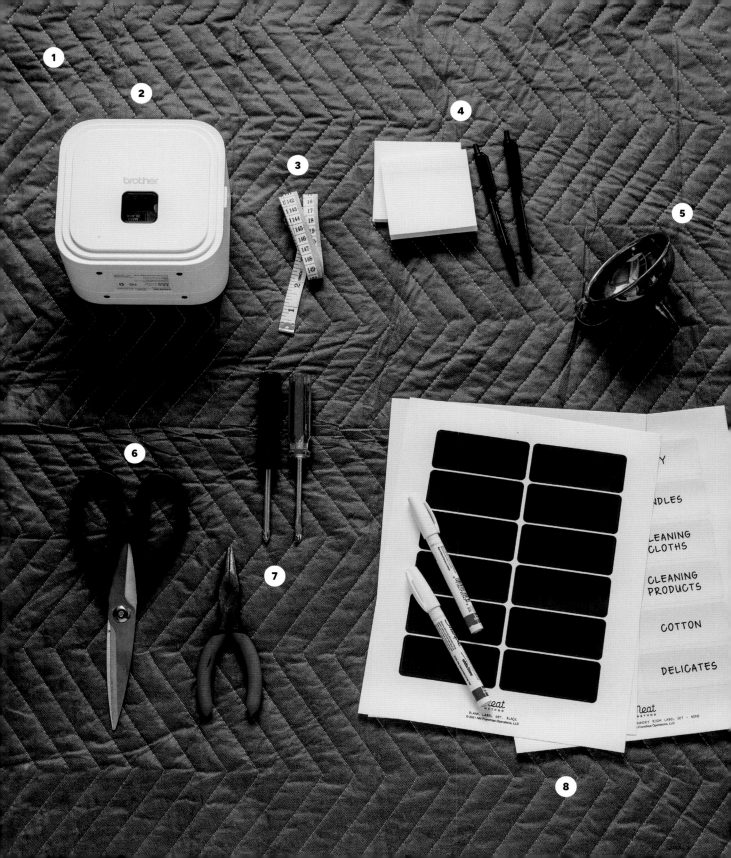

The NEAT Organizing Kit

We love organizational products that are simple and multifunctional, so you can easily repurpose them as your needs and routines change. A home can be expertly organized with bins, drawer dividers, and canisters (these "essentials" are all that most of the recipes in the pages that follow will call for). If you want to go a step further, risers and turntables are also excellent options to improve access to items on shelving and in cabinets.

Note, however, that even though you might feel that purchasing pretty bins is the best part of this process (and we sometimes agree), we strongly advise completing steps 1 through 3 of the NEAT Method process (see pages 14–15) prior to making any container purchases. This way you'll know exactly what quantity, size, and style of organizational products you need. That said, it is useful to have some key items at the ready. Below is the organizing kit we suggest keeping on hand, to ensure that the recipes that follow go quickly and smoothly.

1. **Drop cloths/blankets.** For placing items on when you're emptying a space to categorize them.

2. **Electronic labeler (optional).** For creating uniform labels throughout your home.

3. **Soft tape measure.** For determining the appropriate sizes for organizational products (see A Note on Measuring, page 17).

4. **Sticky notes and pens.** To indicate what will go where when determining a system for the space (we like to write each category on a sticky note and place it where we want the category to "live").

5. **Funnel.** For decanting into coordinating jars (see page 19 for more on decanting).

6. **Scissors (optional).** For various ad hoc uses, including trimming labels to size.

7. **Pliers and/or screwdrivers.** For adjusting shelves to accommodate different heights for storage.

8. **Labeling materials.** For labeling the contents of a designated container. Preprinted label sets are a wonderful tool if you'd like some extra support when creating a system. They are typically available by room, so they can help you select the categories you need.

Glue dots (not pictured). For securing drawer organizers in place.

Shopping or tote bags (not pictured). For sorting items into categories ("Give Away," "Mend," etc.).

Cleaning supplies (not pictured). Dusting cloths and multipurpose spray for giving spaces a quick wipe-down once they're empty.

Kitchen & Pantry

Dish Towels **28**

Cookware **31**

Cooking Tools **32**

Spices **35**

Food Storage Containers **37**

Kids' Tableware **38**

Water Bottles **41**

Refrigerator **42**

Pantry **45**

Snacks **46**

Baking **49**

Morning Routine **50**

Cleaners & Under-Sink
Supplies **53**

Multipurpose Drawer **54**

FOR MOST OF US, the kitchen is the heart of the home—a place where the family gathers, culinary creations come to life, and game nights unfold. Due to its multifaceted role, the kitchen often has the most potential for transformation.

When approaching this space, one consideration eclipses all others: the layout. Our guiding principle is to envision the dishwasher (or your sink if you don't have a dishwasher) as the nucleus of this space, around which all of your daily essentials should orbit. To determine the ideal placement of your kitchen items, we recommend a simple yet effective exercise: stand in front of your dishwasher, open it, and imagine unloading it. The seamless flow of this process should dictate where your most frequently used items find their homes.

FIVE THINGS TO CONSIDER

1 **Cabinet configuration.** Take a close look at your cabinet setup. Do you have upper cabinets, open floating shelves, or a predominance of drawers and lower cabinets? The answer will guide your storage decisions. For example, you wouldn't want to keep storage containers or mismatched dishware out on open shelving, or your heavy everyday items in a bottom drawer that is difficult to access.

2 **Pantry solutions.** If you don't have a dedicated pantry and need to designate an alternative location, identify a space (e.g., a cabinet or drawer or an additional storage area outside of the kitchen) that is still accessible and away from the stove and sunlight to preserve these items.

3 **Most-used appliances.** Identify the small kitchen appliances that you rely on daily—perhaps a coffee maker, blender, and toaster. Ensuring swift access to these items is pivotal for streamlining your morning routine.

4 **Cooking collaborations.** Reflect on how many individuals typically engage in culinary endeavors simultaneously. If multiple cooks share this space, consider creating distinct prep zones to enhance efficiency and harmony.

5 **Kid-friendly accessibility.** If you have little ones, decide what items you'd like them to be able to reach easily and safely. Tailoring certain areas to their needs can foster independence and involvement.

DISH TOWELS

A dish towel drawer is the easiest "quick win" in a kitchen. Use the drawer closest to your sink for efficiency. File folding each towel allows you to see what you have and easily access what you want to use.

APPROX. TIME:
5 minutes

ESSENTIALS:
Spring-loaded drawer divider(s)

1. Editing will be one of the most important steps of this project: confirm that all towels you choose to keep are in good condition and similar in size. Then measure the drawer to determine the size of drawer divider(s) needed.

2. Insert the drawer divider(s).

3. File fold each towel to a width and height that will fit within the divided drawer: Lay the towel flat and fold in thirds the long way. Fold in half by bringing the bottom to the top. Fold in half from bottom to top again to complete the look. Place them in the drawer with the fold upright.

APPROX. TIME:
20 minutes

ESSENTIALS:
Lid rack

COOKWARE

When it comes to storing cookware, it's all about location, location, location. You'll want to keep your pots and pans as close to your cooktop as possible.

1. Determine what cookware you need to store here. Especially if you are tight on space, be very thoughtful about what you actually use on an everyday basis. Oftentimes, people feel they need a "complete" set of pots and pans, which isn't the case. Unless you're a particularly advanced cook, you can probably handle most of your everyday meal prep with a single pot, a frying pan, and two saucepans.

2. Nest the pots and pans and place the lids in a rack.

⬇ If you have enough space, you can store your pots and pans in a deep drawer near the stove with the lids on. Use a drawer divider to keep things from shifting. You may also nest these items and use a drawer divider to hold the lids along the side of the drawer.

Pro Tip

"File" baking sheets in a tall, slim cabinet, arranging them from largest to smallest, or store them in your oven drawer.

COOKING TOOLS

The key to arranging this space is editing. You most likely have unnecessary doubles and triples of things, as well as specialty gadgets that aren't used frequently enough to justify the space they take up in your drawer. When deciding whether to purchase a single-function tool (e.g., a cherry pitter or an avocado slicer), consider two things: how often you will reach for the gadget, and whether you could accomplish the task with a tool you already own.

APPROX. TIME:
20 minutes

ESSENTIALS:
Expandable drawer organizer or spring-loaded drawer dividers

1. Gather all of your kitchen tools and identify any multiples. Ask yourself how many people prep at the same time and which duplicates are used simultaneously, if any. Eliminate any unnecessary duplicates and unused specialty gadgets and sort the remaining tools according to category (e.g., baking, grilling, vegetable prep).

2. Measure the drawer to determine which organizing product to use.

3. Place the drawer organizer or dividers in the drawer, then add the tools, keeping them in their categories.

APPROX. TIME:
1 hour
ESSENTIALS:
Spice jars, funnel, bin, labels
EXTRAS:
Riser

SPICES

How you store your spices will be based on how much you cook. If you are an adventurous chef, then you are going to need to dedicate more space to your spices—perhaps an entire drawer or cabinet shelf. If you aren't, then a small bin on a shelf should suffice. Whichever option you choose, ensure that the spices are in close proximity to your cooking prep area.

1. Gather all of your spices and check their expiration dates. If a spice in your cabinet expired three years ago, get rid of it—and don't replace it until the next time a recipe calls for it. Believe us when we say that if you didn't touch the last bottle in all this time, you're probably not about to use the replacement, either.

2. Determine which size jar will work for all of your common spices, and decant them using a funnel. Store any specialty spices that need to stay in their own containers, such as truffle salt, in a bin and place it on a higher shelf.

3. Determine where you'd like your spice collection to live (on a shelf or in a drawer) before applying labels to either the jar faces or lids. If storing your spices on a shelf, use a riser so all the bottles are visible and you don't lose any at the back of the shelf. Arrange the bottles either by frequency of use (with the most commonly used spices up front) or in alphabetical order.

APPROX. TIME:
20 minutes

EXTRAS:
Spring-loaded drawer
divider or narrow bin

FOOD STORAGE CONTAINERS

Like water bottles (see page 41), food storage containers seem to proliferate all on their own. From mismatched Tupperware to old take-out containers, it's easy to end up with a hodgepodge of items that leave your cabinet in disarray. Simplifying to one matching, nesting set can make a huge difference in how much storage space is required.

---

1. Ensure that every container has a matching lid and that plastic items are free of stains.

2. There are two options for storing the containers: either stack them with the lids attached or nest the containers and group all the lids together.

3. If storing the containers nested, insert a drawer divider or a narrow bin along one side of the space to contain the lids.

← We suggest keeping single-use food storage products near the reusable containers, so everything is in one location. Baggies can be removed from boxes and placed in shallow open drawer organizers or plastic bag drawer organizers. This will enable quick access and cut down on visual clutter.

KIDS' TABLEWARE

First, consider whether these items should be placed where it's easiest for kids or for adults to access them—this will probably depend on the child's age. We recommend using a bottom drawer, to encourage kids to get involved in setting the table. And as with everyday dishes, we suggest placing kids' dishware and utensils near the dishwasher or dish-drying rack to simplify the process of putting them away. This location will be in constant transition as your children age, so we recommend a flexible solution like a drawer divider or bins that can be moved as the items in this area change. (Once the kids start using the everyday tableware, this drawer can be turned into storage for school lunch containers.)

APPROX. TIME:
20 minutes

ESSENTIALS:
Spring-loaded drawer dividers or bins and labels

EXTRAS:
Canister

1. Sort the tableware to ensure that you have sets that are in good condition and still age appropriate.

2. Decide whether to sort by type (e.g., flatware, plates) or by child if your children are of varying ages and needs.

3. Measure the drawer to determine the size of your drawer dividers, or use a labeled bin for each category.

4. Place kids' flatware upright in an open canister alongside the dishes (or store in its own section of your everyday flatware drawer).

APPROX. TIME:
5 minutes

ESSENTIALS:
Spring-loaded drawer
divider(s)

EXTRAS:
Small bin

WATER BOTTLES

Whether we buy them when we take up a new sport, receive them as a gift with purchase, or pick them up at a random event, somehow we end up with far more water bottles than we actually use. To determine how many each person in your household really needs, think about how many times you use one in a week and how many times a week you run your dishwasher. Once you figure that out, organize what remains either by activity or by household member.

1. Ensure that every bottle has a coordinating top and that all components are in working order.

2. Measure a deep drawer to determine the size of your divider(s).

3. Sort the bottles according to your preferred system, insert the drawer divider(s), and place the bottles in the drawer.

4. Consider including a small bin for spare parts like straws or gaskets.

← *If you don't have a deep enough drawer to house your bottles, add a bottle organizer to a shelf, making sure to keep each category (activity or household member) together. This way, instead of some bottles "hiding" in the back of the cabinet, they'll all remain in view and easily accessible.*

REFRIGERATOR

A well-organized refrigerator is essential for maintaining food fresh-ness, reducing waste, and streamlining meal preparation. Whether you prefer to have a fully stocked fridge at all times or buy only the necessities for the week, organizing your fridge can make a significant difference in your daily routine.

APPROX. TIME:
1 hour

ESSENTIALS:
Old sheet or paper, bins, turntables, storage containers

EXTRAS:
Can and/or wine bottle holders

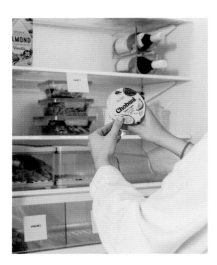

1. Place an old sheet or protective paper on the counter if you have a fragile stone countertop—there are tons of oils and acidic ingredients that can leak from containers. Remove everything from the fridge, checking expiration dates and sorting into categories according to how a grocery store is organized (i.e., dairy, produce, deli).

2. Determine where each category should live in the fridge. Refrigerators come with built-in boundaries: walls, drawers, and shelves. Bins and turntables will further demarcate categories to ensure they don't shift to another area and get forgotten about. We typically discourage highly specific organizers, but can and wine bottle holders can be helpful in preventing drinks from taking over a shelf.

3. Place food back into the fridge by category. Understanding your shopping habits can help you determine how much space to devote to each category within your fridge. Instead of filling it to capacity, start with the essentials.

Pro Tip

Because refrigerators have high turnover, they require frequent upkeep. Before putting away new groceries, take a moment to quickly put items back in their correct places and check for freshness.

PANTRY

Believe us when we say that your pantry might be the most fun space to organize. With the proper preparation and planning, it's one of the most rewarding transformations to achieve. It's also one of the areas that requires you to be ruthless with your editing. If an item is expired, it must go! The easiest way to think of it is, "If I haven't consumed it by its expiration date, chances are I never will."

---

1.   Protect your floors and counters with an old sheet or paper. The oils from pantry products are known to leave marks.

2.   Remove all the items from the pantry space and place them in categories on top of your counters or along the perimeter of the kitchen while you work (for more on categorization, see tip below). Be sure to check expiration dates as you go, discarding anything past its date.

3.   Once each category has been determined, select the size bin or canister needed by measuring the space the items take up. Our number one rule in a pantry is to make things simple and symmetrical. Create a cohesive design story by limiting the number of materials you incorporate throughout the space—we recommend no more than two or three. Take it a step further by limiting size variations on the same shelf. Only one size container per shelf. This not only maintains visual harmony but also makes it easier to refill containers because they are the same size. There's no second-guessing what size refills to purchase when you're out shopping.

4.   Turntables and risers are essential to maximize ease of access. Both ensure nothing is forgotten in the back of your cabinets. Risers are perfect for lining up shorter canned goods. Turntables are great for tall, narrow bottles like condiments. Implement along a shelf that is at or near eye level as needed.

5.   Label each container. This way there's no excuse to not put an item back in its designated home.

← If you're unsure of how to categorize your pantry items, you may want to use a preprinted pantry label set for inspiration. Some suggested categories: baking, breakfast, dinner prep, kids' snacks, pastas and grains, salty snacks, and sweet treats.

SNACKS

Determine how you'd like snacks to be accessed in your home. Should everyone be able to get to all of them, or are there some that you would prefer be out of reach of children? How you organize bulk snacks will depend on how much space is available. If you have plenty of room, you can decant the snacks into canisters. If you are short on space, sort the snacks by category and place them in a bin together.

APPROX. TIME:
1 hour

ESSENTIALS:
Canisters, bins

EXTRAS:
Spring-loaded drawer dividers, labels

1. Separate snacks into those that should be decanted (e.g., nuts) and those that should be individually placed in a drawer or bin (e.g., protein bars). We advise taking individually wrapped snacks out of the box. Determine the size of the canister or bin you need for each category (we suggest long, narrow bins so each category can be lined up and visible at the front of the shelf).

2. Decant all loose, frequently purchased snacks into canisters and place them on a shelf (or in a deep drawer, with the lid labeled). We generally discourage the use of backstock bins, but if the way the snack is packaged requires more space than a canister can offer, use a bin to hold overflow. Categorize individual snacks by type and place them in divided drawers or bins.

3. Label containers or drawers (if you feel that the contents aren't obvious).

Pro Tip

Like the refrigerator (see page 42), the snack zone is an area with high turnover and a lot of daily activity. Consider building in a moment for weekly upkeep when you are creating your shopping list or putting away groceries.

GRAB & GO

SNACKS

SNACKS

BAKING

Are you an avid baker, or do you bring out the mixer only a few times a year? The answer to this question determines how much space you should dedicate to this category, and how close to your prime real estate these items belong (more on this on page 15). It goes without saying that the more often you do something, the more accessible the supplies should be. If you're an infrequent baker, reserve an upper shelf for a single bin of necessities.

---

1. Gather all your baking items and place them on a counter together. Check expiration dates and evaluate which items are worth keeping. (That turbinado sugar you used for a single recipe three years ago? Toss!)

2. Determine two different sizes of canisters that will work for your categories (more than two will cause your cabinet to become visually cluttered). Be mindful that the sizes you choose will inform the quantity of items you can purchase moving forward.

3. Decant package contents into your chosen canisters and label accordingly, being sure to include expiration dates.

4. Collect occasionally used supplies or tools in a bin and place on an upper shelf.

← If you're interested in decanting, we suggest starting with one category that you frequently reach for—maybe sugars or flours. You might end up loving the system so much that you decide to decant everything.

MORNING ROUTINE

Creating a dedicated zone for your morning rituals will allow for a better, more efficient start to your day. Whether this is your coffee, smoothie, or breakfast station, place all the necessary items together within easy reach and start the day off on the right foot.

APPROX. TIME:
1 hour

ESSENTIALS:
Canisters, labels, bin

EXTRAS:
Spring-loaded drawer dividers, turntable

1. Gather all necessary supplies. (For a smoothie station, for example, this could include dry ingredients, glasses, and straws.) Choose a spot in the kitchen that's easy to access and provides enough space for you to complete your routine.

2. Decant loose items into canisters. If you're using a drawer, add dividers to create boundaries. Label all containers accordingly. If you have many small jars or other containers you reach for on a daily basis, consider placing them on a turntable for ease of access.

3. Arrange overflow and occasionally used items in a bin and place it on an upper shelf.

Pro Tip

One trick we frequently use is to dip a bin under the piping. Though the fact that the pipe protrudes into the bin a bit makes removing difficult, it can be a good home for larger items that can be easily grabbed with one hand.

TRASH BAGS

CLEANING PRODUCTS

CLEANING PRODUCTS

CLEANERS & UNDER-SINK SUPPLIES

The space under the sink is one of those areas that can easily turn into a dumping ground—it's hard to get to all the nooks and crannies around the plumbing, and it seems like there is a specialized cleanser for every appliance and kitchen surface. For most homes, the best approach to the under-the-sink area is to use it only to store everyday essentials—you're aiming for an easy grab-and-go experience. (Less frequently used cleansers can be stored in a labeled bin or basket in another location like a laundry or utility space.) We love using long bins in a space like this to prevent items from being lost in the chaos.

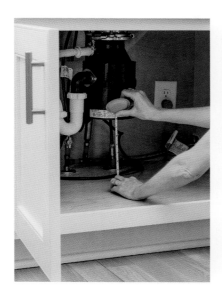

1. To determine what size bins will accommodate your plumbing, measure all areas under the sink.

2. Place the bins in the space. Edit down to the cleansers and other products you use on a daily and weekly basis and sort by purpose.

3. Place the items in the bins and label accordingly, ensuring that the most frequently used products are at the front for quick access.

MULTIPURPOSE DRAWER

We prefer the term "multipurpose drawer" rather than "junk drawer"—but whatever you call it, this is the drawer where random items accumulate. The goal is to enable it to function even if there are products from many different categories within it. When selecting the location of your multipurpose drawer, choose a spot on the periphery of the room.

APPROX. TIME:
1 hour

ESSENTIALS:
Modular or expandable drawer organizers

1. Edit the contents of the drawer down to your essential everyday needs. For example, a small bottle of multipurpose glue could live here, but occasionally used wood glue should not.

2. Measure the drawer and decide how many categories you would like to fit within it. Whether it makes sense to use modular drawer organizers or an expandable one-piece organizer will depend on what you're storing. Typically, smaller items are best stored in individual organizers. Larger items (like writing utensils, scissors, and tape) will fit well in a one-piece insert.

3. Place items back in the drawer, using your organizers or insert to divide them into categories. This will create a flow and calm the chaos of the space. This is a great area to make a habit of touching up monthly. Take a few minutes to remove what doesn't belong and return items to their correct spot.

Pro Tip

If the drawer organizers you select do not have rubber feet, purchase some adhesive ones to attach yourself. This will help prevent the organizers from sliding around when you open and close the drawer.

Bedroom

T-shirts **64**

Sweaters **67**

Workout Apparel **68**

Denim **71**

Undergarments **72**

Shoes **75**

Jewelry & Accessories **76**

Purses & Bags **79**

Closet **80**

Dresser **83**

Nightstand **84**

WE'RE ALL FAMILIAR with the idea that a bedroom should be a sanctuary, a haven of tranquility where you can unwind and truly relax. Yet the stress brought on by chairs heaped with clothing, piles of dirty laundry, and a growing stack of online returns can shatter the sense of calm we crave. This is why we advocate for adopting a "less is more" attitude in the bedroom. This not only simplifies the maintenance of your space but also allows for a focused and serene start to your day, and a less overwhelming end to it.

FIVE THINGS TO CONSIDER

1 **Occupants' lifestyles.** Reflect on who shares the space with you and whether your respective needs and lifestyles differ. Does one of you embrace a collector's mindset while the other prefers a more minimalist approach? Proper space allocation and storage solutions should accommodate these distinctions.

2 **Storage availability.** Assess how much storage space you have in your bedroom, including in dressers and closets and under the bed. Efficient use of these resources is essential for an organized environment.

3 **Seasonal wardrobe.** Determine whether all of your clothing and accessories can be stored in this space or whether other areas of your home need to be utilized (e.g., maybe you'll want to store winter boots elsewhere during summer months).

4 **En suite bathroom.** If your bedroom includes an en suite bathroom, consider how the flow works for your daily and nightly routines. If the bathroom has storage, consider placing pajamas or undergarments in this space for easy access when you come out of the shower or bath. Ensuring a seamless transition between the bedroom and bathroom enhances functionality.

5 **Laundry and cleaning.** Decide where you'll keep dirty laundry and manage dry cleaning. Will it be within the bedroom, in a closet in another room, or in a dedicated laundry room?

Clothing Organization 101

With the possible exception of organizing your kitchen, sorting out your closet and dresser can have the biggest impact on your daily life. Being able to quickly grab what you need each morning, and easily put it away at the end of the day, encourages you to wear what you already own and discourages clutter caused by tossing items on the nearest surface. The following tips can be applied to any clothing storage setup, no matter its size or configuration.

FILE FOLDING

The number one tip of any professional organizer is to file fold, a simple process (shown below) that can be used for T-shirts (page 64), sweaters (page 67), denim (page 71), and more.

There's often a misconception that it is more challenging to maintain this system than to stack clothes or even just toss them into the drawers. The truth is, it's not only easier, but it also allows you to properly see everything you own in a category and to store more items in the space. Be honest with yourself: when was the last time you wore the tee at the bottom of the stack in your drawer? If your answer is "Which tee is at the bottom?" you should be file folding.

To remove or return an item, simply insert your hand like a divider, push the group forward, and slip the item out or in. If there are times between laundry days when the grouping doesn't fill the space and stay upright, simply let the stack lean backward at an angle.

HANGING

We encourage hanging most clothing items (excepting knitwear, which can stretch out over time). No matter what you're hanging, hang it all in the same direction. As well as looking tidier, this will save you seconds each day, which can quickly add up.

What direction the hangers should face depends on how you walk up to the rod: the front of each clothing item should be facing you as you approach the closet. With a walk-in closet, we typically have the hanging items face the left, so that going through them mimics the process of reading from left to right. If you have a larger closet with hanging garments on both sides of a divider like shelving, you may opt to have each side face the shelving in the middle.

COLOR-CODING

Color-coding refers to sorting a group of items by color. Typically, this approach is used with identical or nearly identical items that sit close together and are indistinguishable at a glance. The most frequently color-coded items are clothing and books. But the system can also be applied to linens, board games, even canned goods if that's your vibe.

We like to start with white, follow with pink, red, orange, yellow, green, blue, purple, brown, and gray, and finish with black. To a certain extent, color-coding is a personal preference like labeling. Some people enjoy having everything color-coded. Others prefer a more wabi-sabi, relaxed approach, especially for smaller groupings of items.

COLOR-CODING PATTERNS

Plaid shirts and printed dresses are very tricky because up close there can be what seems like multiple dominant colors. Treat them like a Monet and back up. You need to take in the full picture of the grouping and adjust by what your eye sees from a distance.

T-SHIRTS

It's important to consider your available space and the number of T-shirts you own when deciding whether you should hang or fold them. If you choose the latter option, we strongly encourage file folding and creating boundaries with drawer dividers. It's the best way to see what you have so that you don't always just grab the tee that's on top. Here's how it's done.

APPROX. TIME:
20 minutes

ESSENTIALS:
Spring-loaded drawer dividers or bins and labels

1. Determine the width of the space available and the number of rows that will fit across the drawer or bin. Add drawer dividers if necessary to maintain rows. To begin file folding, lay the shirt face down on a flat surface and fold the first side in. Repeat with the second side, so the width fits the available space.

2. Fold in half from top to bottom.

3. Fold in half from top to bottom again, so the shirt is folded into fourths. Once all the tees are uniformly folded, color-code them (see page 62) and place them in the drawer or a labeled bin with the fold upright.

Pro Tip

If your folding skills aren't up to par, consider using a folding board to help you master the technique.

Pro Tip

A folding board can be discreetly stored alongside a stack of sweaters and is really helpful when trying to create symmetrical stacks.

APPROX. TIME:
20 minutes

ESSENTIALS:
Shelf dividers, spring-loaded
drawer dividers, or bins
and labels

SWEATERS

We encourage folding any delicate or heavy sweaters so that they retain their shape. Shelf dividers are an excellent way to maintain stacks of sweaters on shelves. We suggest using dividers made of acrylic, so they don't create visual clutter. If you decide to place your sweaters in labeled bins, run your hands along the inside of the bins to make sure that the material there will not snag the sweaters.

1. Determine the width of the space available and the number of rows that will fit across the drawer, bin, or shelf. Add drawer dividers if necessary to maintain rows. To begin folding, lay a sweater face down on a flat surface. Fold in the sides, so the width matches the available space.

2. Once both sides are folded in, take the bottom and fold to the top. Repeat so the item is folded into fourths.

3. Once all the sweaters are uniformly folded, color-code them (see page 62) and store them with the fold upright.

WORKOUT APPAREL

Workout gear can be one of the hardest categories to keep organized. Not only do workout clothes often look similar, but they are also constructed of materials that are structureless, making them difficult to keep folded. The trick is to keep them contained rather than aim for perfection.

APPROX. TIME:
20 minutes

ESSENTIALS:
Spring-loaded drawer dividers or bins and labels

EXTRAS:
Under-bed bin

1. One way to cut down on the chaos is to limit the number of workout outfits that you own to the number of days per week that you work out (i.e., if you work out twice a week, keep only two or three full outfits).

2. File fold the items that remain (see page 60 for more on this technique). If you choose to store your workout clothing in a drawer, add drawer dividers. If you want to use bins on a shelf, consider labeling each one individually, so you can separate tops from bottoms and specialty from everyday gear.

3. Rather than mixing workout apparel in with your everyday clothes, you may want to store it under the bed or in a closet or cabinet nearest to where workouts take place.

Pro Tip

Because swimwear is structureless, like workout apparel, we suggest storing it in a bin. If you have a lot of two-piece or strappy suits that cannot be nicely folded, you may opt to place them in individual storage bags that can then be placed in the bin.

APPROX. TIME:
20 minutes

ESSENTIALS:
Hangers, spring-loaded
drawer dividers, or bins
and labels

EXTRAS:
Shelf dividers

DENIM

We recommend stacking denim on a shelf, file folding it in a drawer, or hanging if space allows, with the pairs color-coded (see page 62). However you choose to store your jeans, make sure they are folded so that a back pocket is out. This makes it easier to identify a particular pair. If stacking on a long shelf, it's nice, but not necessary, to add shelf dividers. This will help keep the stacks upright. Also be thoughtful of how high you stack the denim. The higher the stack, the harder it is to access the bottom pair.

1. If storing on a shelf or in a drawer, determine the width of the space available and the number of rows that will fit across. Add drawer dividers if necessary to maintain rows. To begin folding, lay a pair of jeans face up on a flat surface. Fold in half lengthwise with the back pockets facing out, and tuck in the upper inseam. Be sure the width matches the available space.

2. Fold in half in the opposite direction. If you are going to hang your jeans, place them on hangers now.

3. If you are storing your jeans on a shelf or in a drawer, fold them in half again, so they are folded into fourths. Once all the jeans are uniformly folded, place in a drawer, on a shelf, or in labeled bins with the fold upright.

UNDERGARMENTS

Boundaries and ruthless editing are key to taming undergarment drawer chaos. This is an area where people often keep way more than they actually need or even wear. The undergarment drawer can benefit from a "uniform" approach: purchasing only one type of sock or underwear enables you to quickly get ready in the morning.

APPROX. TIME:
20 minutes

ESSENTIALS:
Spring-loaded drawer dividers, bins

1. Pull out all of your socks, underwear, and bras. Discard any with holes or other wear and tear, "orphaned" or unmatched socks, and ill-fitting garments. Sort the remaining items and assess where you might have unnecessary duplicates—for example, ten pairs of black dress socks when you need a pair only every once in a while.

2. Depending on how much space you have, consider pulling out your occasional-use items (such as those for formal attire or to go under a particular garment) and placing them in a bin on a higher shelf in your closet. This can create some much-needed space.

3. Add structure to the drawer. We suggest using either drawer dividers or bins that are designed to be placed in drawers. This will help create boundaries between various categories.

4. Place the garments back in the drawer, file folded (see page 60) and grouped like with like. Even socks can be filed: just fold them in half and organize according to color (if you wear only one type and color, it's perfectly okay to ball them up and toss them in, as long as there's a strict boundary like a drawer divider). We like to nest underwire bras like at a shop, so they don't become dented. Bralettes can be laid flat.

SHOES

We always advocate keeping items within a category together, so you know exactly what you have and you don't overbuy. Shoes can be an exception to the rule: you may have everyday shoe storage near the main entrance of your home in addition to in your bedroom, as well as less accessible storage for off-season or special-occasion footwear. Just make sure there's a rhyme or reason to what lives where, or you run the risk of forgetting what you have and not wearing it.

---

1. Determine which shoes you wear most often (this can vary greatly by season) and group them by style. For example: everyday, formal, sneakers, and sandals. Stack less frequently worn shoes in individual clear or labeled lidded shoeboxes and move them to a space outside the prime real estate. Typically, this is a higher shelf that's out of immediate reach.

2. Place the remaining shoes on shelves or a shoe rack facing forward, sorted by category and then by color, with the lightest colors at the top and the darkest at the bottom. (Face one shoe forward and one back *only* if necessary to allow for an additional pair to be stored. This system does not create visual calm.)

3. Boots should never be hung. Place them flat in a bin, or use boot shapers to maintain their upright position on the floor or on a shelf.

⬇ *To save on space, we love to "file" sneakers and sandals in open bins with the heels down and toes up, then place the bins on the floor of the closet or on a shelf.*

JEWELRY & ACCESSORIES

We love to organize jewelry in open trays, so you can see what you have—which will make it more likely that you wear it. If you put on the same couple of pieces every day, they could be placed in a trinket dish on your nightstand (see page 84) so you can easily remove them at night and quickly grab them in the morning.

(see page 84)

APPROX. TIME:
1 hour

ESSENTIALS:
Drawer organizers or Ultrasuede or linen (for lining the drawer)

EXTRAS:
Bin, jewelry safe

1. The first step when organizing jewelry or accessories is to sort by frequency of use. Everyday accessories such as a beloved watch or favorite belt should be stored in an easy-to-reach "prime real estate" zone, such as a top drawer or eye-level shelf.

2. If you're using drawer organizers, select options with a padded or smooth lining, so jewelry doesn't get scratched. If you decide to lay jewelry directly in a drawer, use a shallow top drawer and line it with Ultrasuede or linen purchased from a fabric shop.

3. If you are tight on space, you might want to invest in a separate storage bin for seasonal items like heavier scarves or special occasion pieces. You might also consider purchasing a small jewelry safe to store any high-value or heirloom pieces.

➡ *You may opt to display your hats if you have a curated collection (be sure to follow care instructions for proper placement). Otherwise, they can be kept in a bin nested within one another. More structured hats should be stored in hatboxes to keep their shape and protect them from dust.*

HATS

PASS

APPROX. TIME:
20 minutes

ESSENTIALS:
Bin(s), paper sorter,
or shelf divider

EXTRAS:
Bag stands

PURSES & BAGS

There are generally two approaches to storing bags: display them on a shelf or store them away. We strongly encourage the former, if your space allows. We find that if they are tucked away, you are less likely to use them. If you don't want to display your bags, they can be stored in a bin on a high closet shelf (when empty, they are typically light, so it's not difficult to reach overhead for a bin).

1.   If you have limited space for bags, consider dedicating the prime real estate to everyday bags. Then store formal, vacation, or seasonal bags in a bin on a higher shelf.

2.   Use a paper sorter to keep clutches and wallets upright and "filed"— many stores sell an acrylic version that can hold three to five. A shelf divider can serve the same purpose. Alternatively, these items can be stored upright in a bin.

3.   When it comes to unstructured bags, consider utilizing bag stands to help maintain their shape.

Pro Tip

If you like, fill each bag with a bag pillow, or create one by filling the bag's dust bag with crumpled tissue paper, to help the bag retain its shape. If the bag did not come with a dust bag, you can place lightly crumpled tissue paper directly in the bag.

CLOSET

The clothes closet is where you start and end your day, and it can make you feel either motivated or completely overwhelmed. We have found that establishing a proper system can reduce stress and create more time to do the things you enjoy most.

It's a misconception that you need to edit your belongings before you consider organizing. The truth is, editing should take place only after you've had the chance to group together the items in all of your categories. How else are you going to realize that you own fifty white tops, several of which are too "well-loved" or you no longer wear?

APPROX. TIME:
Full day

ESSENTIALS:
Hangers, bins, spring-loaded drawer dividers or organizers

1. Remove everything from the space and sort into categories. Are any clothes kept in other areas of the home or off-site? If so, take note of those items as well. Perhaps some should be moved back into your main closet or some seasonal or special-occasion items should be moved to storage.

2. Discard any "well-loved" items. Set aside items that need to be tailored or are ready for donation/consignment. Edit out unnecessary duplicates, clothing that never gets worn, and whatever quantity is causing overflow.

3. Analyze which categories will fit best in each section of the space. We generally suggest hanging as much as you have room for (except knitwear), as hanging is the lowest-maintenance approach to keeping things visible and tidy. Keep in mind that whatever you wear most should be granted the prime real estate. Also consider whether you should dedicate shelves to items that you love seeing on a daily basis. If you are a passionate collector of hats or bracelets, consider putting these items on artful display rather than stuffing them away in a bin.

4. Swap out mismatched hangers. Place items back in the closet, using bins and drawer dividers or organizers as needed, and with all hangers facing the same direction and garments color-coded from light to dark within each category. (For more on this, see page 62.)

Pro Tip

If you also have a dresser, consider tackling it at the same time to help in determining how best to divide up your categories (see page 83 for more on organizing this space).

APPROX. TIME:
4 hours

ESSENTIALS:
Spring-loaded drawer
dividers or drawer organizers

EXTRAS:
Folding board

DRESSER

Dressers are one of the most useful pieces of furniture you can employ to add storage to a bedroom. However, they can either make or break efficiency in your daily routine, depending on proper setup and upkeep.

1. Remove everything from the drawers. Set aside items that need to be tailored or are ready for donation/consignment. Discard any "well-loved" items that cannot be donated. If you transition your wardrobe with the seasons, now would be a good time to separate out any items that should be stored until the next transition.

2. Sort what remains into categories, such as undergarments, pajamas/ loungewear, short-sleeve tees, long-sleeve tees, workout apparel, sweatshirts, sweaters, swimwear, and jeans. With your items sorted and in front of you, take the opportunity to ensure that you don't have any unnecessary duplicates. Keep only what you actually enjoy wearing: don't waste precious space on clothing that never gets worn. If you regularly struggle with closing your drawers, you may also need to edit down further for the sake of space—be realistic about how many items you can comfortably fit, and don't purchase more without culling first.

3. Determine what will be stored in each drawer. Often the top drawers of a dresser are narrower and work better for smaller items like jewelry, undergarments, and socks. The next drawers down could be home to tees, workout clothes, and/or pajamas. Bottom drawers are good candidates for heavier items like sweaters, sweatshirts, and pants.

4. Measure each drawer and determine the number of rows that can fit across it. Add drawer dividers or organizers if necessary to maintain rows.

5. Complete the file-folding process (for tips by category, see pages 64–72). Try your best to make each fold as uniform as possible. If your folding skills aren't up to par, consider using a folding board to help you master the technique.

6. Color-code (see page 62) by category, stacking the rows with the lightest items placed at the front left corner of the drawer and the darkest at the back right corner.

NIGHTSTAND

Much like a multipurpose drawer (see page 54), nightstands often accumulate random items. But they can be a great option for extra storage—we suggest storing pajamas there in bedrooms without dressers. The top drawer should be reserved for nightly essentials, though. A pretty tray or trinket dish on top of the nightstand can hold a watch or ring that's removed only before bed, or lip balm that you frequently reach for in the middle of the night.

APPROX. TIME:
20 minutes

ESSENTIALS:
Drawer organizers

EXTRAS:
Decorative tray or trinket dish

1. Remove everything from the top drawer and decide whether it all truly belongs in your bedroom. Essentials might include lip balm, tissues, lotion, an eye mask, a notepad and pen, chargers, and headphones or earplugs.

2. Now it's time to play a version of Tetris: place everything on a flat surface and group the items into categories. This will allow you to determine what type of modular configuration will be necessary to corral loose items within each category and prevent them from sliding around.

3. Measure the drawer to determine how many inserts will fit. Too many, or too many different sizes, will disrupt the visual calm you're trying to create.

4. Place the organizers in the drawer and add your nightly items.

SHAMPOO & CONDITIONER

BANDAGES

Bathroom & Linen Closet

Everyday Essentials **90**

Makeup **93**

Linen Closet **94**

Sheets **96**

Towels **98**

Medication **101**

First Aid Supplies **102**

Guest Bathroom **104**

Travel Toiletries **107**

BATHROOMS AND LINEN CLOSETS often pose an organizing challenge due to their limited size and the multitude of products we tend to accumulate within them. Linen closets in particular often become unruly areas of a home if left unmanaged. While the term "linen" suggests a specific purpose, in reality, these closets often serve as a catch-all for bathroom overflow, travel essentials, paper goods, and even first aid items.

However, there are two simple principles that can restore order: pare down and keep only what you truly need, and establish effective systems that will not only help you visualize and access your essentials but also assist you in identifying items you no longer need or want. Analyzing the layout of your bathroom and identifying your daily needs, using the considerations on the opposite page to guide your thinking, will enhance the functionality of your space and significantly streamline your morning and evening routines.

THREE THINGS TO CONSIDER

1 **Storage options.** Do you have a dedicated linen closet? Is there a medicine cabinet that you can utilize for storing small items?

2 **Users.** Who uses the bathroom regularly? If it's a family bathroom, you'll need to make it kid-friendly, and choose storage locations while considering the children's needs and safety. In bathrooms with multiple sinks, designate specific sides for different users. This can help keep personal items organized and accessible.

3 **Safety.** Make sure that medicines and first aid supplies are placed out of reach of children and stored securely.

EVERYDAY ESSENTIALS

The key to organizing everyday essentials is ensuring that you've pared down to the staple products and tools you truly use every day. Once you've finished editing, store everything that remains as close as possible to where you perform your morning and evening routines. Nothing should be more than an arm's length away.

APPROX. TIME:
4 hours

ESSENTIALS:
Bins, labels, drawer organizers, canisters, spring-loaded drawer divider(s)

EXTRAS:
Turntables, tray

1. Remove all of your products and sort them by category. Categories to consider include body care, feminine hygiene, hair care, nail care, oral care, and skin care. Eliminate any expired products and those you no longer use.

2. Within each category, separate your everyday products from those you use occasionally and backstock. Be sure to label backstock bins so that you remember what you have and it's easy to access when you need it.

3. Place everyday items in your prime real estate. For example, dental products tend to be small and should be put in small drawer organizers and placed at a higher level. Keeping like items together, store those that are not for everyday use in a separate location where they won't take up valuable space.

4. Hair-care products tend to take up the most real estate, so consider a larger bottom drawer or under the sink in bins or on turntables. Because hair tools are typically longer, store them in a divided bin with canisters to allow for upright storage, which will make it easier to quickly grab them. Additional options are adding one or more dividers to a drawer to help contain items and placing products on a turntable.

5. For drawers that need to contain multiple categories, add open canisters. There's no need for a lid because they are already in a drawer. Adding a drawer divider will minimize shifting.

6. Use the counter as your last resort! Consider a tray to corral beautifully packaged products or those you use every time you're in the bathroom, and pretty lidded containers to store single-use items such as ear swabs.

Pro Tip

Most cosmetics have an expiration date. You can typically find a small symbol that looks like an open jar with a number followed by the letter "M." That is the number of months the product is good for once it has been opened. This is also called the PAO ("period-after-opening") symbol.

APPROX. TIME:
20 minutes

ESSENTIALS:
Drawer organizers

EXTRAS:
Makeup brush cup

MAKEUP

If cosmetics are your love language, then you'll want to invest in individual drawer inserts. Make sure to select ones that can easily be cleaned and that fit in the drawers or on the shelf you have available. For additional space, consider storing makeup brushes in an attractive cup on the counter.

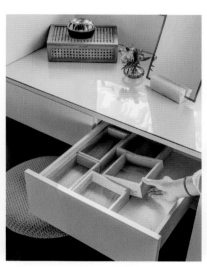

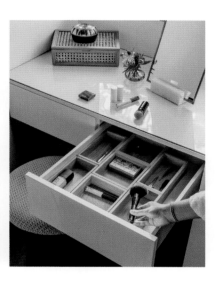

1. Collect all of your makeup products. Group like items and purge anything that is past its shelf life (see tip, opposite) or that you don't use. Due to their small size, it makes sense to store cosmetics in a shallow drawer for ease of access. Wipe out the drawer and measure for organizers.

2. Placing the organizers is like solving a puzzle—play with the configuration until you figure out an arrangement that works with your specific products and available space.

3. Return each category to the drawer in its own insert. Because makeup has an expiration date and tends to get messy, it makes sense to periodically maintain the space. Do a quick sweep every six months to eliminate expired products and clean the containers.

LINEN CLOSET

A disorganized linen closet can be a real pain because it's tough to quickly distinguish one sheet or towel from another. Therefore we strongly encourage containing everything in bins. This will ensure that even if household members "toss" items back in the closet, at least they will still be properly categorized.

APPROX. TIME:
1 hour

ESSENTIALS:
Bins, labels

1. Determine what needs to be stored in your linen closet. Can it be used only for linens, or does it need to be a multifunctional space? Some common items to keep in a linen closet are bathroom categories that don't fit in that space (such as medications or first aid), utility items such as light bulbs or batteries, and paper products.

2. After determining what should stay, sort into categories and designate a bin or bins for each category.

3. Identify your prime real estate. Place items that you reach for on a daily or weekly basis, such as linens and bathroom items, on the shelf at eye level.

4. Place the heaviest or bulkiest items at the bottom of the closet, such as occasionally used beach towels.

5. Place your infrequently used but lighter items on the top shelf. These items should definitely be in a bin to make them easier to grab and so they don't get lost at the back of the shelf.

6. Label each bin. For bed linens, consider labeling with the mattress size or the name of the person who uses them.

Pro Tip

If your home is not equipped with a dedicated linen closet, keep a single spare set of sheets in each bedroom and store spare towels in each bathroom.

SHEETS

Determine how many sets of linens you genuinely need for each bed in your home. Having one or two extra sets for emergencies (or young children) or guest use is usually sufficient.

Once you've determined what you need, pull out all of your linens and ensure that every set is complete (top sheet, bottom sheet, and requisite number of pillowcases) and in good shape. Then uniformly fold the linens, following the steps below for fitted sheets, to establish visual consistency. (For instructions on folding towels, see page 98.)

<table>
<tr><td>APPROX. TIME:
20 minutes</td></tr>
<tr><td>ESSENTIALS:
Bins, labels</td></tr>
</table>

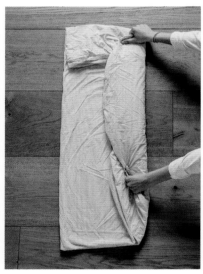

1. Start with the sheet long and vertical. Fold the sheet in half horizontally, tucking the rounded elastic corners into each other.

2. Fold the sheet in thirds: bring the rounded tucked corner to the center and fold the other side over that, creating straight vertical sides.

3. Fold in thirds vertically, bringing the bottom third to the middle, followed by the top third. You should now have a long rectangle with straight edges only. Continue to fold in halves until the sheet can fit in the designated bin (labeled if you're organizing them by room or size).

TOWELS

Towels are quite bulky and quickly take up valuable space. Before deciding whether you want to stack them on a shelf or store them in bins, you should consider how many towels you truly need. Being strict with yourself in this category can go a long way. If a towel is dingy, it has to go! Matching sets can make a world of difference when it comes to feeling organized.

We love folding towels so that only the fold is facing out. This allows for visual calmness and makes grabbing one towel so easy.

APPROX. TIME:
5 minutes

EXTRAS:
Bins, labels

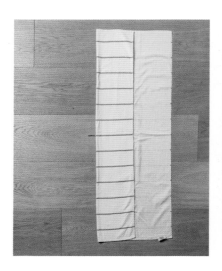  

1. Lay the towel flat and fold in thirds the long way.

2. Fold in half in the opposite direction

3. Fold in half again to complete the look. Stack on a shelf with the fold facing out or place fold up in bins (labeled if you want them divided by room or type).

APPROX. TIME: 20 minutes
ESSENTIALS: Bins, labels
EXTRAS: Turntable

MEDICATION

Consider creating space in a linen closet (or bathroom) for your medication. Storing medicines in multiple areas of the home leads to overbuying and products expiring before they're used up. It is also advised to keep medication away from excessive humidity created by showers, as well as from light and heat. We recommend keeping only a small amount of what you may need and steering away from bulk buying in this category.

---

1. Check expiration dates and properly dispose of any expired or unneeded medication (see tip, opposite).

2. Divide medication by over-the-counter versus prescription, adult versus child, as well as type of treatment (cough, fever, upset stomach, etc.).

3. Place the different categories in labeled bins or arrange them on a turntable. If children live in the home or are regularly visiting, ensure that all medication is placed out of reach.

4. Consider storing daily supplements and/or vitamins in a small bin near your morning routine essentials in the kitchen (see page 50). It is easier to remember to take them if you see them every day.

FIRST AID SUPPLIES

APPROX. TIME:
20 minutes

ESSENTIALS:
Canisters, bin, label

Create a first aid kit that can be carried wherever it's needed. This can be accomplished by simply storing items in a bin together or purchasing a ready-made kit.

Unlike toothpaste or toilet paper that you know you will use daily, a first aid kit is something you will hopefully not have to reach for very often! So that nothing unexpectedly expires, have on hand only what you need, and only in small amounts. Bandages can lose adhesiveness when they get too old, and over-the-counter medicines can quickly lose their potency.

---

1. Gather your supplies—a standard kit may include twenty-five adhesive bandages (in assorted sizes), antibiotic ointment, topical antiseptic, two packets of (81 mg) aspirin, an instant cold compress, two pairs of large non-latex gloves, hydrocortisone ointment, thermometers, and tweezers.

2. Place canisters in a labeled bin to divide the available space. Fill each canister with a different category (e.g., bandages, ointments, medicine, instant compresses, gloves, and small instruments/tools). You can use canisters with lids to prevent dust, but we like to keep them off to expedite grabbing what we need.

3. The bin should be placed out of the way but in a spot that's easy to access. Think a shelf higher than the one you use for your daily items but that you can reach without a step stool. A guest bathroom or mudroom on your home's main level might even be a great idea. If you have children and live in a larger home, it may make sense to have a kit on each floor.

Pro Tip

The American Red Cross has helpful lists of what to keep on hand based on the members of your household. See redcross.org/get-help /how-to-prepare-for -emergencies.

FIRST AID

GUEST BATHROOM

The function of a spare bathroom should be to provide a space that's welcoming to guests. Anticipating what someone may need helps with planning out this space—in addition to towels, think extra toilet paper, feminine hygiene products, a spare toothbrush, toothpaste, dental floss, hand lotion, a nail-care kit, and hair-care products. As a bonus, while you don't want to turn your spare bathroom into a storage space, these items can essentially double as backup products for your own personal use.

APPROX. TIME:
1 hour

ESSENTIALS:
Canisters, drawer organizers, or bin and label

1.   Collect the products you'd like to offer your guests. Think about the items you most frequently forget to pack or you wish you had but don't want to ask for when visiting a friend or family member. As much as possible, select items that are individually packaged or hygienically appropriate to share.

2.   Divide the items by category and place them in separate canisters, then place the canisters in an obvious location like an open shelf or on top of the vanity. If you don't have counter or shelf space, create a guest drawer with the top, easiest-to-access drawer. Implement drawer organizers to create boundaries for different categories. Guests will be able to quickly find what they need without going through multiple drawers. You could also place a selection of items in a bin labeled "Be Our Guest."

3.   Some guests might feel uncomfortable opening cabinets to look for what they need, so we suggest also placing a stack of washcloths and hand towels out where the guest can see them.

4.   When a guest ends their visit, touch up the space. A few minutes of upkeep to replenish and put away items will give you one less task to complete while preparing for your next visitor.

ESSENTIALS:
Dopp kit/travel toiletry case,
bin, label, canisters

TRAVEL TOILETRIES

Travel toiletries can quickly get out of hand. For some reason, it's often the free stuff that's hardest to part with. Like tote bags piled up in a coat closet, sample toiletries can take over valuable storage space. Remember, they were most likely complimentary! Create a firm boundary and stick to it.

---

1. Gather together all of your travel-sized products and pare them down.

2. Keep your Dopp kit fully stocked at all times—that way it's always packed and ready for travel. Depending on how often you travel, this can either live with your everyday toiletries or have its own dedicated space.

3. Use a reasonably sized bin to hold everything not stored in your Dopp kit, sorted by category (e.g., hair care, skin care, dental care) in lidless canisters (as with First Aid Supplies, page 102). If products start to spill out, it's time to edit. Place the bin on a higher shelf out of the way. There's no concern with forgetting about the bin because packing for a trip will always trigger your need to access it.

Pro Tip

Rather than buying travel-sized products, purchase reusable travel containers and fill them with your everyday products.

Kids' Spaces

Closet **112**

Dresser **115**

Books **116**

Stuffed Animals **118**

"Treasures" **121**

Playroom **122**

Legos **125**

Dress-Up **127**

Art Supplies **128**

Kids' Artwork **131**

Homework Station **132**

CREATING ORGANIZED KIDS' SPACES is not only enjoyable but can also alleviate the overwhelming feeling that often accompanies the multitude of items involved. In designing a child's space, the priority is to establish a straightforward system that even children can effortlessly maintain. And be sure to take the opportunity to plan for the future, ensuring that your system can adapt and evolve with your child's changing needs.

You want to create not just a functional and organized space but also an environment that nurtures your child's growth and independence.

FOUR THINGS TO CONSIDER

1 **Child participation.** Assess how much your child can engage in the organizational process. If they are old enough to comprehend the objective, involving them can be a valuable learning experience. It instills a sense of responsibility and ownership over their space.

2 **Independence.** Define the tasks you want your child to undertake on their own. Setting up designated areas where they can access and put away toys fosters self-sufficiency and promotes tidy habits from an early age.

3 **Toy storage.** Determine where the toys will be stored. Many families prefer not to store toys in the bedroom, especially for toddlers. This separation of play and sleep areas can aid in establishing routines and maintaining a clutter-free sleeping space.

4 **Future sibling planning.** Consider whether there's a need to strategize for the storage of items that may be handed down to a future sibling. Ensuring a seamless transition of toys and belongings between siblings can simplify the process when the time comes.

CLOSET

Like other kids' spaces, closets are frequently in a state of transition. At the newborn stage, the closet is mostly used to store diapers, next-size-up clothing, and toys. Once a child is in elementary school, you'll want to make space to hang their clothing. Determine what you want your kid to be able to access at lower levels and set up the space accordingly.

APPROX. TIME:
Full day
ESSENTIALS:
Bins, hangers
EXTRAS:
Size dividers

1. Remove everything from the space and sort it. If toys are also stored here, ensure that categories have not outgrown their containers. If they have, consider editing or moving them to another location, like a playroom or a different area of the bedroom.

2. Set aside any clothing and/or toys that children have outgrown to be donated, or place them in a storage bin for a younger sibling. (For more on this, see tip below.)

3. This is also the time to swap old hangers for new. It makes a notable difference to use baby and/or adolescent-sized hangers, so the clothes stay on them and don't get stretched out.

4. Place all hanging items back in the closet, facing the same direction (for more on this, see page 62). For babies and toddlers, who fly through sizes, consider adding size dividers. These labeled rings fit on the rod and help you keep things sorted. Organize hanging items by type, and then color-code each type (see page 62). If it's a double-hung closet, the traditional approach would be to hang tops on the top rod and bottoms on the bottom; for younger children who might not be able to reach a higher rod, consider hanging everyday clothing on the bottom rod and special-occasion clothing on the top rod.

→ *There's nothing more frustrating than grabbing an outgrown onesie for the third time during a diaper change. Designate a "Too Small" bin on a higher shelf in your child's closet to set aside the clothing until you have the time to stow it away for a younger sibling, give it to a family member or friend, or donate it. (This same concept applies for items that are too big, whether those are hand-me-downs from an older sibling or gifts the child hasn't yet grown into.)*

HATS

WINTER ACCESSORIES

SPORTS

Pro Tip

For closets with a single hanging rod, include a small step stool for elementary school–age kids to encourage independence.

APPROX. TIME:
4 hours

ESSENTIALS:
Spring-loaded drawer
dividers

EXTRAS:
Labels

DRESSER

Dressers offer a great opportunity to encourage independence in children. When they are young, consider putting everyday items like underwear and socks in the bottom drawers, so they can easily reach these items on their own. As they grow through different developmental stages, incorporate their feedback into the organizational system. Do they like only one type of sock? Lean into that. Buy one type and color and make laundry day easier by just tossing the loose socks into the drawer. Or if getting a child out of the house with socks on always means a trip back to their bedroom, consider moving the socks out of the dresser and placing them in a small bin near the door. With kids, it's all about meeting them where they are and picking your battles.

1.   Begin with an edit. Ensure that everything is the correct size. Are there next-size-up items stored away that should be incorporated? Are there "well-loved" items that need to be mended or recycled? Or any other items that your child doesn't enjoy wearing (let's be honest, refuses to wear) and that should be handed down to a younger sibling or friend?

2.   As with adult clothes, we encourage file folding (see page 60) tees and pants so it's easy to see what you have. Because the clothing is smaller and you can typically fit multiple rows in one drawer, add drawer dividers to keep things neat.

3.   Labeling the drawers can be a big help for occasional caregivers, especially with younger kids who aren't as knowledgeable about what's kept where.

← Instead of buying specialty baby furniture, a low dresser can serve as a changing table and then be converted to a "big kid" dresser as your child grows. Just place a changing pad on top with a small bin alongside for diaper-changing essentials. File fold burp cloths and other items and place them in a top drawer, so they're close at hand during a rambunctious diaper change.

BOOKS

Organizing books for kids is an ongoing process based on their age, their reading ability, and your family's habits. Remaining flexible is key in creating a great system for your budding reader.

APPROX. TIME:
1 hour

ESSENTIALS:
Portable bin

1. Begin by corralling all of their books in one location. Their bedroom is always a great option for a nighttime reading area. (We also love keeping a selection of books in a portable bin to transport to other rooms of the home if we find that the child doesn't always love reading in one location only. Periodically rotate out the books with ones that are stored in the bedroom.)

2. Select storage. For younger children, use the bottom shelves of a bookcase or shelving unit for books they can access themselves. For elementary-school-age and older children, use the entire shelving unit.

3. Create a system. Engage your child when deciding on the organization strategy. The younger they are, the simpler it should be. For pre-readers, books could be organized by color, as children this age typically locate books by their cover rather than by looking for the title. Middle readers and young adults may want to organize by genre (e.g., graphic novels, fiction, nonfiction) and then alphabetically by author or title.

⬇ *So that library and/or schoolbooks don't get lost in the main collection, consider designating a special bin (or even a tote bag) for them.*

STUFFED ANIMALS

APPROX. TIME:
20 minutes

ESSENTIALS:
Oversized bins or hampers

When it comes to stuffed animals, it's best to create a boundary and stick with it. Other than the cherished handful that live on the bed, the furry friends can be limited to what will fit in one or two oversized bins or hampers.

1. Choose a bin style that complements the decor of the room. Open bins are the best bet because they allow for quicker cleanup. Very small children might benefit from bins made with soft materials in the event that they drag the bins along the floor.

2. Once the stuffies start spilling out of the bins, it's time to edit down the collection until it fits again. There are a couple schools of thought when it comes to editing stuffed animals—you either include your child or do it without their knowledge. If you opt for the latter, bag the toys up and store them for a bit in case the child asks for them. There's a good chance that as long as you don't take the beloved friends that live on their bed, they won't notice that the others are missing and after some time passes you can safely donate them.

Pro Tip

As your household grows, create a keepsake bin for each family member. Purchase lidded plastic bins (to best protect contents) and label with each person's name. Periodically adding new items to the bin can be a fun walk down memory lane for everyone.

APPROX. TIME:	
20 minutes	
ESSENTIALS:	
Bin or lidded box, drawer organizers, or display shelf	
EXTRAS:	
Plastic bin for keepsakes	

"TREASURES"

"Treasures" is a beloved NEAT term for children's knickknacks—acorns from a walk, trinkets from a birthday party goody bag, participation medals. It's important for a child to collect treasures, but it's equally important to create boundaries for how large the collection can grow.

1. Designate a space for these treasures in the child's room. It could be a bin, a lidded box, or a drawer in their desk that has been divided into smaller compartments. You could even hang a shelf to display their most cherished items.

2. Periodically edit the collection with your child when it outgrows the space allocated. Certain items will eventually be deemed trash. Important "milestone" treasures can be moved to a larger keepsake bin (see tip, opposite).

← *Just as parents offer open-ended play activities to encourage creativity, we like to suggest open-ended, flexible storage for kids' rooms. You never know when the next passion will take hold. Instead of going out and purchasing a new container, select something that can be used in different ways. A simple container with a lid will hold endless iterations of treasure collections from toddlerhood to the teenage years.*

PLAYROOM

Playrooms are really fun, but organizing them can be a bit overwhelming, between the number of items that need to be categorized and, potentially, children at different ages accessing the space. The good news is that with the proper system, you *can* have a tidy playroom, and your kids can actually learn to do the cleanup!

APPROX. TIME:
Full day

ESSENTIALS:
Bins, labels

EXTRAS:
Canisters

1. Determine what storage options are possible in the space. Most playrooms don't have enough vertical storage. We highly recommend investing in a closet system, furniture piece, or shelving unit with cubbies that will provide vertical storage for the various categories of toys and games you'll want to store here.

2. Sort out items your kids are no longer playing with and those with broken or missing parts. You'll be surprised how much this can eliminate. Dispose of or donate these items. (Tip: this should become a cyclical process as your kids continue to grow and collect more toys. "One in, one out" is a great rule!)

3. Begin organizing by separating each category. Think broadly so that the categories can evolve as the children grow (plus, when categories are too specific, it will slow down cleanup, which no one wants). Here are some of our most frequently used categories: transportation (cars, trucks, trains), dolls or friends, Legos, blocks, puzzles, and games.

4. Once you've compiled each category, you can determine the number and size of storage containers you will need. Remember, simple and symmetrical is the motto—keep to just one or two sizes, and one or two container types. Place your larger, heavier categories in big bins at the base of the storage area and then build up to lighter categories. (That said, ensure that all safety measures are taken into consideration—you don't want kids scaling the shelving for a favorite toy at the top!) For smaller beloved categories, it's nice to place a few decorative canisters within the child's reach for ease of access.

5. Labeling in a playroom is key! Not only does it allow for easy cleanup, but it also helps children with their literacy skills. For young children, consider picture labels.

thanks for the view, mr. mies ←

JENGA

Old Maid
CARD GAMES

DOMINOS

VEHICLES

MUSIC

FRIENDS

BLOCKS

APPROX. TIME:
1 hour

ESSENTIALS:
Canisters or bins with lids

EXTRAS:
Labels, freestanding drawer
unit or open floor bin

LEGOS

How you organize Legos will depend on how your child likes to use them. If you have a builder who enjoys the freedom of grabbing components at will, place their unsorted Legos all together in one open floor bin. Select an attractive bin that can be left out where they like to build. If you have a precise builder who has specific ideas about what they want to create, organizing by color is a great way to foster that creativity. We have found that the color-coding method allows children to pick up the instruction books that come with their sets and sift and sort for the exact pieces they need in a particular color.

1. The most labor-intensive part of this project is sorting the pieces by color. This is the perfect time to get your children involved in the organization process. The more hands, the easier it will be to accomplish. Although it's time-consuming, the reward is worth the labor.

2. Once you've determined the number of colors you're working with, select canisters or bins (preferably clear) in just one or two sizes. (Don't use more than two or the variation will throw off the symmetrical vibe we're going for here!) If you're using opaque containers, add a label to each one.

3. Store the containers stacked neatly on shelves and within reach of your child, to foster independent play and cleanup.

APPROX. TIME:
1 hour

ESSENTIALS:
Hangers or a decorative wall hook system, bin

DRESS-UP

For kids, dress-up isn't only for Halloween. Embrace their spirit of imaginative play and create a designated home for dress-up items. We strongly suggest creating only one space in the home for them, to ensure that they're actually used.

1. This is a category that you'll want to frequently edit. Halloween is a perfect time for an annual overhaul, as new costumes will help replenish the dress-up collection. Pass down any that are too small to friends and family, set aside any that need mending, and discard any that are beyond repair.

2. Once you've culled the collection, there are two main ways to store children's dress-up clothes: If your child has enough closet space, you can dedicate a lower bar to costumes and hang them. Alternatively, hang a row of hooks on the wall at their height for quick access.

3. Be sure to incorporate a bin for accessories. There's no need to be too precious with these items. You want to give your kids the freedom to play and the ease to independently pick up when playtime is over.

⬅ *If you know your child doesn't have the patience to rehang items, then be practical and toss everything into a bin or hamper.*

ART SUPPLIES

Art supplies can become disorderly very quickly. Along with putting things back where they belong, set aside time regularly to purge the items that have dried up, are empty or broken, or are missing caps or lids. As with most systems, once you have created order with your art supplies, a little maintenance is all that's needed to keep things neat. If you don't have shelving available for an art-supply zone, we love using a three-tiered rolling cart. It can be pulled out when needed, then tucked away in a closet when not in use.

APPROX. TIME:	1 hour
ESSENTIALS:	Canisters, bins, labels
EXTRAS:	Tiered rolling cart, paper sorter, lidded box

1. Start by sorting and editing your current supplies. Determine whether anything needs to be restocked, thrown away, or donated.

2. Identify supplies that you are comfortable with your kids accessing at any time. Use plastic canisters with lids to store these in individual categories. Paper can be placed in either a bin or an acrylic paper sorter. If you have the space, dedicate a small bin or envelope to craft and paper scraps that can be used for future projects.

3. Next, set aside the supplies you do not want children using unsupervised. Place these items in a box with a lid or in a labeled bin and store it on a shelf out of immediate reach. This will ensure that you know when these supplies are being used and can keep an eye on things. Finally, place coloring and activity books together in a labeled bin.

ARTWORK

Connor

CONNOR'S BOOK OF ART

FINN'S BOOK OF ART

EXTRAS:
Art book service,
art portfolio, or
weathertight bin

KIDS' ARTWORK

Let's get real: there's only so much room on the fridge. Not all artwork can be kept (or *should* be kept—we said it so you didn't have to). The key to this project is creating a convenient landing spot for incoming projects, then getting into the habit of reviewing and recycling on a consistent basis.

---

1. Designate a "landing zone" for new artwork. This could be a bin in the child's room next to where they unload their backpack, a bin in your garage where artwork gets placed straight after school pickup, or a bin in the kitchen where family paperwork is "processed."

2. Once the bin is full, sit down and go through it. Rather than consider each individual piece, review artwork in bulk. Children frequently go through phases. It's easier to select the first and maybe favorite of their frog watercolor period when looking at them all together. It's much harder when considering each individual piece as it's presented to you. Set aside only a few (or none) and recycle as much as you can.

3. Sort the remaining items by school year or age. At milestones (the end of a school year, a birthday, or a new calendar year), we like to work with an art book service that will photograph the desired masterpieces, then send you a completed book. Alternatively, you could designate an art portfolio, or even a weathertight storage bin, for each child and add the accumulated art once you hit a new milestone.

HOMEWORK STATION

A dedicated space for doing homework can motivate kiddos and save everyone time and energy. Having all their tools and supplies at their fingertips can make for more efficient and better work. If you aren't able to create a dedicated desk area, having canisters and bins stocked and stored nearby to pull out onto a kitchen table or island works great, too.

APPROX. TIME:
1 hour

ESSENTIALS:
Canisters, drawer organizers, bins, labels

EXTRAS:
Paper sorter

1. Corral the supplies your kids typically need. Think beyond pencils and erasers to construction paper and craft supplies—anything they regularly use to complete their work.

2. Use canisters to separate commonly used pencils, markers, and scissors for easy access on a shelf or desk. Drawer organizers are also an excellent way to compartmentalize supplies.

3. Use labeled bins or a paper sorter to separate writing paper from craft paper.

4. The end of the school year is the perfect time for an annual overhaul of this space. Ensure all items are in working order and in full supply. You can also transition it into a temporary art or activity space to keep summer boredom at bay.

Pro Tip

If you have more than one child using the space, it can be helpful to create one bin per kid (labeled with their name), particularly if they work on the same homework packet throughout the week.

Laundry

Detergents &
Laundry Tools **138**

Laundry Systems **141**

Lost & Found **142**

DOING LAUNDRY often occupies a significant amount of our time. In fact, though the laundry is one of the smaller areas of a home to organize (and as such, there are just three "recipes" in the pages that follow), the right setup ensures that we can approach this essential task in a way that makes it more manageable and even somewhat enjoyable. Whether you have a spacious walk-in laundry room or a compact laundry closet or cabinet, the key to conquering this chore lies in simplicity and ease of access. By addressing the considerations on the opposite page and customizing your space to your needs, you can make this time-consuming chore more efficient and approachable.

FIVE THINGS TO CONSIDER

1 **Accessibility.** A well-organized laundry space should have all the necessary supplies at hand. Avoid having to reach high for items or run to another room to retrieve essentials.

2 **Dedicated space.** Is this space designated solely for laundry, from start to finish? Creating a dedicated laundry area helps maintain focus and efficiency, minimizing distractions.

3 **Challenges.** Identify your primary laundry roadblocks. Is it folding clothes neatly, or needing more room for laundry baskets? Knowing your pain points can help you tailor your laundry space to address these specific issues.

4 **Hanging and air-drying.** Consider how you manage clothing items that require hanging or air-drying. Having hooks or racks in your laundry space can simplify this process and keep things organized.

5 **Ironing and steaming.** If you iron or steam clothes as part of your laundry routine, make sure you have a designated area or equipment set up for this purpose.

DETERGENTS & LAUNDRY TOOLS

Laundry routines can vary greatly. Are you someone who has a different detergent for every type of wash? Do you subscribe to all the various stain removers and tool kits for clothing care? However elaborate or streamlined your laundry routine, you'll want to have everything you need within arm's reach. Ideally, laundry tools would be stored near your laundry machines. If you don't have a dedicated room—or even a closet—for laundry, keep these items together in a portable bin that can be easily accessed and moved near your machines.

APPROX. TIME:
1 hour

ESSENTIALS:
Canister or soap dispenser, bins, decorative container or turntable

EXTRAS:
Small bottle, label, collapsible laundry basket

1. Begin by decanting any bulk detergent into a storage container and placing it in the prime real estate in your laundry room (such as on a countertop). You might use a canister for dry powder or a dispenser with a pour spout. Occasionally used cleaning agents can be stored in their original containers in a cabinet rather than decanted.

2. Place smaller, specialty detergents in a bin or decorative container or on a turntable that properly fits the space for easy access. For example, the decorative bin pictured opposite is long but narrow, leaving adequate countertop space for folding.

3. Next, gather items used for ironing and steaming (e.g., distilled water, spray starch), fabric care (lint roller, fabric shaver, sweater stone), and stain removal (including a brush to pretreat stains prior to washing). You should store each of these categories where you complete the task—near a utility tub or the sink nearest your laundry machine, perhaps. (Consider decanting a small amount of pure bleach into a well-labeled bottle for ease of use.) Typically, a small bin is enough to hold everything you need. An ironing board can easily be slipped behind a door if you do not have the closet space available.

4. In terms of the laundry itself, if you don't have space for multiple laundry baskets, consider purchasing ones that nest or even a collapsible one that can be slipped next to your machines.

⬇ Place tools such as wool balls, sweater stones, and lint removers in clear lidded canisters so you can see everything and keep them dust free.

APPROX. TIME:
1 hour

EXTRAS:
Hampers, flat surface,
laundry baskets, bins, labels

LAUNDRY SYSTEMS

As we discussed earlier in this chapter, knowing your challenges is essential to determining a successful system for laundry in your home. Take a moment to consider where your current system breaks down. Is it collecting dirty items? Switching loads? Folding? Putting clean clothes away? Once you've identified your pain point, work with everyone in your household to figure out a solution. Here are four strategies we've introduced in clients' homes.

---

1.   If household members have trouble getting dirty clothes to the laundry room hamper, add one to each bedroom. This means multiple hampers to empty, but it's easier than chasing down dirty clothes from room to room.

2.   To make it faster to move through loads, sort the dirty clothing into labeled bins as it enters the laundry area. The number of categories you sort into will depend on the space you have. Some suggested categories are whites, darks, delicates, athletic items, and linens. Separate dry-clean-only items from regular laundry.

3.   If folding is a dreaded task, create a more enjoyable workspace, whether that means taking everything to the dining table for more room or incorporating a flat surface in or near your laundry machines.

4.   To ease any difficulties with getting clean clothing back where it belongs, add a labeled bin for each household member to the laundry area. Once a week they are tasked with taking their laundered items back to their rooms.

LOST & FOUND

One of our favorite laundry organization tips is to create a "lost and found" area in your laundry space. This is for items that can become permanently "lost" if they are not properly dealt with in the moment, since it's not always possible to immediately return an item to where it belongs.

APPROX. TIME:
20 minutes

ESSENTIALS:
Small bin and label, small canister

1. Place a labeled small bin near your laundry machines where you can toss misplaced items, as well as a small canister for coins and paper money.

2. Once the bin is full or when you have some extra time, like on the weekend, take the bin with you and return the items to where they belong. Consider textile recycling for any lone socks.

3. At the end of the year (or whenever it's full), empty the canister of loose change and put it toward a charitable donation or household outing.

Pro Tip

Where in your home has good light? Store a mending kit nearby, containing small scissors, a needle or two, and thread in common colors like black and white.

Pacific Natural *At Home* jenni kayne

Dirk Denison **10 Houses**

Interiors | Atelier AM

NAPKINS

Storage & Utility Spaces

Home Office & Paperwork **148**

Keepsakes **151**

Personal Tech **152**

Pet Supplies **155**

Utility Items **156**

Entertaining Supplies **159**

Hobbies **160**

Gift Wrap **163**

Reusable Bags **164**

Luggage & Travel Gear **166**

Holiday Decor **169**

Overnight Guest
Accommodations **170**

WHILE IT'S PRETTY SAFE to assume that every home has a kitchen, a bathroom, and a bedroom space, this chapter delves into areas of organization that may not be universal. Your available "extra" living space and your personal priorities will significantly influence how you organize the categories that follow, and, in some cases, whether you maintain them in your home at all.

Maybe you have an entire room dedicated to gift wrapping; if you're living in tighter quarters, perhaps you simply opt to purchase gift wrap as needed. Similarly, we've addressed home offices here even though we acknowledge that many people don't have a dedicated room for one. The organizing principles that follow are adaptable, however, so the insights in this chapter can be applied to the categories that matter most to you.

FOUR THINGS TO CONSIDER

1 **Priorities.** Reflect on whether the categories that follow align with your lifestyle and whether they merit a dedicated space in your home. Is it worth sacrificing some room in your coat closet to store seasonal holiday decorations? Or should you pare down what you have?

2 **Storage space.** Assess the additional storage space available to you and how it can best accommodate the categories you've chosen to prioritize. Are you making good use of vertical space? Could shelving go higher to accommodate empty luggage?

3 **Optimal location.** Determine where it makes the most sense to store each category for easy access and functionality within your home. Are you the type of person who needs something to be immediately accessible in order to remember that you have it? As much as possible, store items in the room that you will use them in.

4 **Frequency of use.** Think through how often you need to access items within each category to streamline your organization approach. If you rarely go through your keepsakes, can they be kept in a less convenient location to create more storage space for items you need on a weekly or monthly basis?

HOME OFFICE & PAPERWORK

A home office is an area that can quickly get out of hand. Personal paperwork alone can be daunting, since most of us have everything from medical information and birth certificates to tax documents and insurance records. If your home office is currently the site of other personal items like long-term keepsakes, and those items are overwhelming the space, consider moving these into another storage area in your home.

APPROX. TIME:
Full day

ESSENTIALS:
Hanging file folders, labels, file storage

EXTRAS:
Envelopes, drawer organizers or pencil cup and tray

RECOMMENDED LOCATIONS:
Home office, kitchen cabinet, top shelf of entry closet

1. First, assess how much paperwork really needs to be kept. Most documents—like health, banking, and pay records—can be accessed online. You can turn documents and receipts from companies that don't have an online presence into PDFs using an app on your phone. And once you are done with taxes for the year, consider putting all relevant documents in a labeled file folder or envelope and placing them in long-term storage. (Typically you only need to keep these for three years after filing, though there are certain situations that require you to hold on to them for longer.)

2. Once you've culled your paperwork to the material that really needs to be kept, you can determine the appropriate filing system. Depending on how much you're storing and your available space, you may want a large filing cabinet, something that rolls in and out of the closet, or just a few movable filing boxes that can be grabbed off a shelf.

3. Next, organize your everyday supplies—pens and pencils, notebooks, printer paper, stamps, and stationery. Limit the supplies to what you actually need (toss out all those promotional pens and dried-up Sharpies!).

4. Arrange your desk or workspace so that these daily essentials are within arm's reach. If you have drawers, measure them and decide how many categories you would like to fit within each one. Smaller items typically do better in smaller individual organizers. Keep the categories broad enough that it's quick and easy to put items back. If you don't have a desk drawer, add a pencil cup and tray on your desk for the items you grab most.

⬇ *When labeling files, we like to left-justify all labels. Not only is this more visually cohesive, but it also makes it easier to scan all the folders at a glance.*

Pro Tip

For security reasons, don't create a "Personal" file in your file cabinet to hold your social security cards, passports, etc.—use a word like "Inspiration." Or store them in a fireproof document box.

Pro Tip

There are many services
that will digitize photos for you.
If you have a large collection that
you don't have space for, store
the most important images in an
archival-quality photo album
or storage box and
digitize the rest.

ASHLEY'S
KEEPSAKES

LAUREN'S
KEEPSAKES

SUMMER 2023 **ELLE DECOR** Nº291
FOOD&WINE JULY 2023 ICONS & INNOVATO
JUNE / JULY 2023 Summer
VERANDA JULY-AUGUST 2023
VOLUME 18 ISSUE 2

RECOMMENDED
LOCATIONS:
Home office, bedroom
closet, attic, basement

KEEPSAKES

Keepsakes are items that evoke special, memorable moments—anything from a baby's receiving blanket to concert ticket stubs. We always encourage creating a "keepsake" category in the home because of the lovely experience of going through it from time to time. However, if the size of your keepsake collection creates stress for you, then it's possible you don't need it all.

1. Your keepsakes may be tucked away all over your home. Start by gathering everything to begin sorting.

2. Choose categories that make sense for you; we recommend making a separate keepsake pile for each person in the family or sorting by decade or significant life milestones. Perhaps you'll want to separate family heirlooms to pass down to future generations.

3. If it feels like there's too much to keep (due to limited space or general overwhelm), don't be afraid to pare down these items. Think about why you kept each item and whether the memory is significant enough to justify the real estate. This can take some energy and might be emotional; give yourself grace and time to process sentimental items. Consider taking photos and reaching out to relatives who might cherish the items before donating or discarding them.

4. Once you've narrowed down your piles, measure the largest item in each category in order to decide what size bins you will need (taking into account the measurements of your intended storage location as well, of course). If you are storing them in a space that's not climate controlled, like a garage or attic, we recommend weathertight bins to protect your items from moisture, dust, and more.

5. Label each bin with your chosen category (e.g., "Riley's Keepsakes" or "High School").

PERSONAL TECH

Technology is now a daily necessity, but no one wants to see devices scattered on every surface in their home. The amount of available space you have and your knack for identifying the different cords will determine how you organize them. If you are a frequent traveler, buy duplicate cords and store them in your luggage in a smaller portable tech organizer so you aren't stuck buying duplicates while on vacation. (If you're an international traveler, include any necessary outlet converters here, too.)

APPROX. TIME:
20 minutes

ESSENTIALS:
Bin, label, canisters, cord wraps

EXTRAS:
Cord labels or painter's tape

RECOMMENDED LOCATIONS:
Kitchen (in a multipurpose drawer or a "command center"), home office, utility storage area near tools

1. Gather all personal tech devices, charging cords, and accessories in one place. Sort by type and use, if that's helpful for your household.

2. Bundle cords by coiling them and securing them with cord wraps. There are options with snaps, Velcro, and twist closures. Label each cord if you have trouble distinguishing them—you can purchase cord labels or write on a small piece of painter's tape.

3. Corral all cords and all adapters together in canisters and place them in one side of a divided bin. Use the other side of the bin to store personal tech devices.

TECH

PET SUPPLIES

We love to create systems that make completing pet activities and chores as efficient as possible. This is a category where it's worth it to spend a bit of money on specialty organizational products if they make caring for your animal friends easier or more enjoyable.

---

1. Determine where you complete your pet routines and clear out a nearby space (such as a shelf, hook system, or drawer). If using a shelf, add small bins to accommodate different categories (e.g., food, treats, leashes, bags, vitamins, toys, bowls). You may want a few canisters to hold treats and/or rolls of dog bags. If using a drawer, measure it to determine the size of your drawer divider. You may wish to create subcategories with canisters to corral smaller items.

2. If your pet eats dry food, consider decanting it into an airtight food-safe container with an easy on-off lid and a measured scooper. It's so much more pleasant than reaching your arm down into a half-empty bag of kibble (and keeps odors at bay)!

3. If your pet requires medicine and you have small children, be sure to store this out of reach or in a childproof container.

4. Consider creating a secondary area in the garage or mudroom for items used for outside play/walking/grooming—any activity that's better suited for outdoors. One or two hooks should suffice, but a small bin could also be used to contain the items. If you don't want to drill into the wall to add a leash hook, consider a heavy-duty adhesive option like a Command hook.

UTILITY ITEMS

Utility storage can mean many things depending on how much storage you have in your home. This category might include emergency supplies, light bulbs, batteries, backstock of single-use paper goods (napkins, paper towels), specialty cleaning supplies, and basic indoor tools.

APPROX. TIME:
1 hour

ESSENTIALS:
Bins, labels

RECOMMENDED
LOCATIONS:
Storage closet, shelving
unit in basement or garage,
laundry room, mudroom

1. Take stock of what you have on hand. We strongly recommend purchasing only your true necessities and only as much as can actually fit in your allotted space. Not every home can handle Costco-sized quantities.

2. Determine what size storage bins you'll need. This is a space where you'll really want to prioritize using matching or coordinating containers. Utility storage can quickly become visually chaotic with the different shapes and packaging of the items being stored. Matching containers will create calm.

3. Because this space isn't accessed every day, it can be easy to forget what goes where. Even if you don't like the look of labels, this would be the space to use them. You'll want to ensure that everything can be quickly found the next time your lights go out!

Pro Tip

In homes with limited storage space, stack uniform lidded bins to take advantage of any vertical space on shelving.

APPROX. TIME:
20 minutes

ESSENTIALS:
Bins, labels

EXTRAS:
Shelving unit

RECOMMENDED LOCATIONS:
Credenza near patio entrance, storage space near kitchen

ENTERTAINING SUPPLIES

If you're an entertainer, create a space that can hold anything and everything you need for a special occasion: platters, bowls, outdoor dishware, even ice buckets and coolers. This space can also accommodate items for al fresco entertaining or ones you take with you on picnics or to the beach.

1.   Gather everything you use for entertaining. Removing these items from the kitchen can free up precious space for everyday dishware and cooking tools.

2.   Sort into categories by type and use. You may want to designate one shelf for items you use at home and another for items to bring on excursions.

3.   Determine where you'll store what according to frequency of use. The most-used items should be at eye level. Keep heavier and bulkier items toward the bottom of your storage area and other less frequently used supplies at the top.

4.   Implement bins and label as needed. Oftentimes, dishware—especially oversized platters and punch bowls—does not benefit from organizational products. Instead, simply line up items so you can easily see and access everything. We discourage nesting more than two or three bowls or platters because they can get heavy, and as a result become difficult to access.

← *If you frequently eat outdoors, consider creating space in a piece of furniture near your patio door for quick access to items like napkins or outdoor dishware.*

HOBBIES

Hobbies are an excellent outlet for creativity, calm, and relaxation. In order for them to be truly enjoyed, though, the items you need for these activities should be organized in a way that makes it easy for you to access what you need. If it takes too many steps to get to the items, you'll avoid the activity.

APPROX. TIME:
1 hour

EXTRAS:
Bins, specialty storage items, trunk organizer, tote or bag

RECOMMENDED LOCATIONS:
Home office, top shelf of coat closet, storage cabinet closest to where you do your hobby, car trunk

1.   Make a list of everyone in the household's current hobbies. If a family member no longer pursues a particular hobby, donate the items related to it. (You may not even realize how many hobbies you have tried over the years!)

2.   Corral the things you use for each activity in one location. Pull out duplicates, toss anything that is no longer functioning, and do any other necessary editing.

3.   Now that you've narrowed down to the items you truly use, it's time to figure out where they will be stored. Most people do not have the luxury of a room dedicated to crafting like Martha. Hobbies need to be mobile—easily pulled out when time allows and put away so everyday life can resume. If you have a hobby that is enjoyed at home, gather supplies in a bin near where it happens. If you enjoy your hobby outside your home, you might need to invest in specialized gear to transport everything. A trunk organizer can be used to hold everyday needs in addition to sporting goods; gear bags with wheels also work well for sports equipment. If you play role-playing games or paint en plein air, purchase a tote or a bag that can be stored in your coat closet and easily transported to its destination.

→ *Puzzles and games should be stored near a table. If you don't have the space for multiple irregular boxes, consider taking the puzzles and game components out of their original packaging and creating a cohesive system. Each puzzle or game can be put in a zippered pouch, and then they all can be stored in a bin together.*

APPROX. TIME:
1 hour

ESSENTIALS:
Small zippered pouch, bins,
vertical or under-bed gift
wrap organizer

EXTRAS:
Canisters, decorative
upright container, turntable

RECOMMENDED
LOCATIONS:
Laundry room, mudroom,
home office, coat closet

GIFT WRAP

Creating one location for all gift wrap will keep things efficient when you are rushing out the door for a neighborhood party or kid's birthday bash.

1.   Gather all of your gifting supplies. These may include gift bags, gift wrap, tissue paper, ribbon and bows, cards, and gift tags. We love to include a small zippered pouch that contains a roll of tape, scissors, and a pen or two, so you don't have to track them down when you're wrapping a gift.

2.   Once you corral all of your supplies, it will be easier to decide on the type of system you need—one bin for everything, or several bins and canisters. If you have a lot in this category, consider separating holiday from everyday gifting supplies (i.e., hostess, thank-you, and birthday gifts) so that your everyday bins are easily accessible but the rest can be taken out and put away at each holiday.

3.   Rolls of wrapping paper can be stored in a vertical gift wrap organizer or in an under-bed version. If you have the space, store rolls in an upright container (like a decorative trash can)—something simple and at least 14 inches tall to accommodate the length of the rolls. This looks inviting and makes for a lovely experience when grabbing what you need.

4.   If you have the space, a few small bins or canisters on a turntable are excellent for sorting and storing wrapping accents like ribbon and bows. Just be sure that whatever you use allows for enough space so bows don't get crushed. Otherwise, a lidded bin large enough to hold all the items is perfect to store in a closet. You can also place the pouch containing scissors, tape, and the like in the bin.

Pro Tip

If you are tight on space, consider keeping your supplies in the laundry room, where your folding area could be used as a gift wrap area when needed.

REUSABLE BAGS

We always find it funny how something that is typically free can be so difficult for many people to edit. Reusable bags and tote bags tend to pile up and spread out into different areas of the home. The goal for this category is to set boundaries.

APPROX. TIME:
5 minutes

EXTRAS:
Bin, label

RECOMMENDED LOCATIONS:
Garage, entryway, coat closet, mudroom, pantry

1. We suggest doing this a bit backward. Purchase one bin that fits the space you have to store these bags, or designate a drawer for this purpose. Edit your current collection with this space in mind. As you sift through your bags, pause on each one and ask yourself whether you will ever use it, and how.

2. Tuck handles into each bag before file folding (see page 60; aim for the same shape for all the bags, if possible).

3. Return the stack to the bin or drawer; label the bin, if using.

LUGGAGE & TRAVEL GEAR

Storing luggage can be challenging due to its bulkiness and weight. If you're a frequent traveler or share your household with multiple family members, you may find yourself facing an array of different-sized suitcases in need of a practical solution. The key is to centralize your luggage storage to eliminate the frantic search for a particular suitcase. Following are four additional space-saving tips for tackling this category.

1. To maximize space, place smaller pieces of luggage inside their larger counterparts. (This is a benefit of purchasing a luggage set, because sets are typically designed to nest together.)

2. For households with multiple members, it can be beneficial to invest in the same type of suitcase for everyone. This uniformity not only simplifies identification but also streamlines storage: since all the suitcases share the same dimensions, they can efficiently occupy a single space.

3. Utilize your luggage itself for additional storage. You can stow packing cubes, travel pillows, or any other travel-specific gear right inside your suitcases. This not only helps conserve storage space but also ensures that you have your essentials ready when it's time to pack for your next journey. (Store travel toiletries in your bathroom or linen closet, though—as discussed on page 107. These items can expire before your next trip, so it's wise to keep them in a separate, easily accessible location.)

4. As much as possible, it is beneficial to store like with like. If you have the space, dedicate an entire storage area to bags and/or travel equipment. Use bins to hold sleeping bags, travel pillows, hiking backpacks, and even school backpacks during the summer.

APPROX. TIME:
4 hours

ESSENTIALS:
Weathertight bins

EXTRAS:
Wreath containers or bags, string light dividers, anti-tarnish cloth or bags, labels

RECOMMENDED LOCATIONS:
Garage, basement, attic, storage closet

HOLIDAY DECOR

Seasonal and holiday decorations often pose a unique challenge when it comes to organization. These items can quickly take over your garage or storage space, and unlike neatly stackable items, many of them have irregular shapes and sizes and don't fit precisely in bins or on shelves. The real trick here lies in your ability to be ruthlessly honest with yourself about which items you genuinely use and need to keep. It's crucial to be pragmatic about the storage space you have available and to make choices that align with that reality.

---

1. Gather all seasonal decor from various storage areas in your home and garage. Seeing everything together will help you quickly identify excess and edit unneeded items.

2. Categorize all items by holiday. Toss anything that is "well-loved" or broken and donate any items that no longer match your aesthetic. Items that hold sentimental value but aren't actually used for decor should be stored with keepsakes (see page 151).

3. Determine the best space and type of storage for these items. Opt for weathertight storage if you're keeping these items in a location where they may be affected by water or moisture (e.g., garage, basement, attic). This is one category where we acknowledge that specialty storage can be preferable to general bins—seasonal wreaths can be stored in plastic wreath storage containers or bags, string lights should be wrapped around a plastic divider and filed in a bin, and silver pieces should be stored in anti-tarnish cloth or bags.

4. Consider labeling the entire inventory of each bin for ease of placement when it's time to decorate, then group bins by holiday.

5. Larger items such as freestanding yard decorations will likely need to stay on the ground. Designate an area that is out of the way of the main traffic flow.

Pro Tip

While colored bins for different holidays and seasons are popular, we prefer all clear matching bins for a clean aesthetic and ease of viewing contents.

OVERNIGHT GUEST ACCOMMODATIONS

It takes only a few steps to make a guest feel truly welcome in your home. Even without a dedicated guest room, you can create a warm and inviting experience for them. Personalize what you offer each guest to show that you were really thinking about them when preparing for their arrival.

APPROX. TIME:
1 hour

ESSENTIALS:
Hangers, bins, catch-all tray

RECOMMENDED LOCATIONS:
Guest bedroom or closet nearest to where guests will be sleeping

1.   Temporarily clearing a shelf, drawer, or some hanging space and providing a few hangers is a lovely gesture. Consider removing extra personal items or clutter, especially if your guests are staying in a shared space like a home office. Store these items in a bin out of the way, then replace them once the visit is over.

2.   Arrange the following on the bedside table: a catch-all tray for jewelry and keys and a "Be Our Guest" bin containing all the essentials they may have forgotten while traveling, plus a few "nice-to-haves" to create a comfortable stay (think tissues, shower essentials, basic toiletries, a hairbrush and hairdryer, and a USB charging block). If space allows, consider including a water carafe or bottled water and a glass.

3.   In a large bin or shelf in the closet, gather extra pillows and blankets, fluffy bath linens (washcloth, hand towel, and bath towel), and a comfy robe.

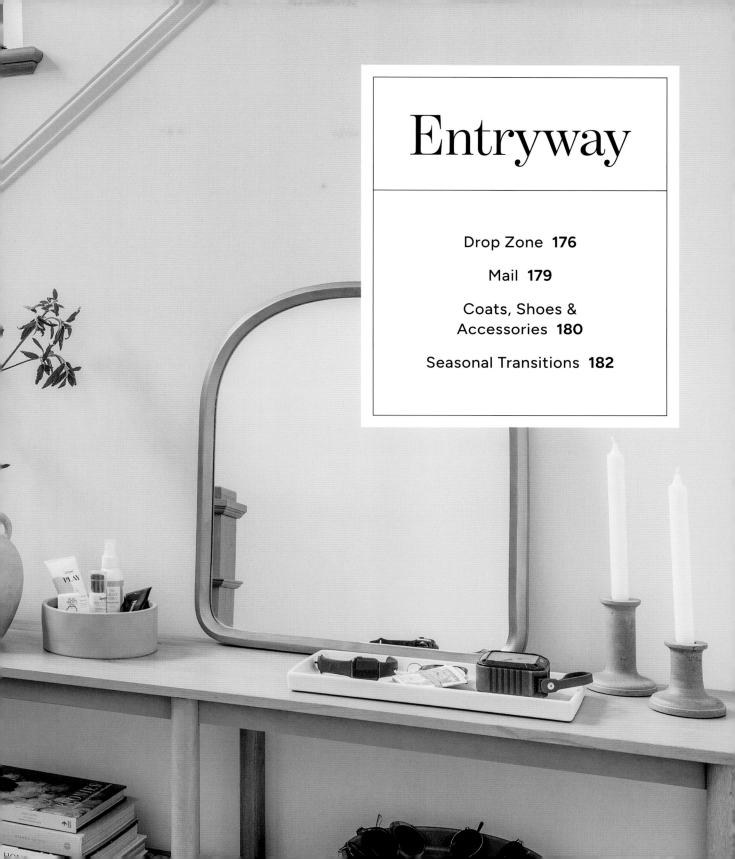

Entryway

Drop Zone **176**

Mail **179**

Coats, Shoes &
Accessories **180**

Seasonal Transitions **182**

AMONG ALL THE SPACES within your home, the entryway holds a distinct honor—in this often compact yet bustling area, efficiency reigns supreme. Crafting a well-organized entryway not only maximizes this modest space but also sets the tone for those first steps out the door each morning.

FOUR THINGS TO CONSIDER

1 **Easing the morning rush.** This space should be the epitome of "grab and go." Reflect on what might hinder your swift exit when you're dashing out the door. Are there any areas that tend to slow you down or create unnecessary chaos?

2 **Keeping essentials at hand.** Identify the items that you or your family members routinely need as you leave the house. Ensuring easy access to these things streamlines your daily routine.

3 **Storage solutions.** Evaluate whether your existing storage options suffice or if you need to invest in purpose-built solutions such as a console table, shoe rack, or coatrack to enhance functionality.

4 **Clutter control.** Take note of the items that habitually find themselves scattered when you reenter your home. Creating designated spaces for these items can effectively curb entryway clutter.

DROP ZONE

A drop zone is a dedicated area in your entryway that holds the essential items you need to quickly exit your home each morning (think keys, sunblock, sunglasses). It should be a small space, but if organized properly, it will make all the difference in your daily routines.

APPROX. TIME:	1 hour
ESSENTIALS:	Drawer organizers, bins and labels, or decorative trays
EXTRAS:	Bench, hook

1. Gather all items that the members of your household typically grab before leaving. Include only the things you need every day—the idea here is to make everything visible and easily accessible. Then sort by use or person.

2. If you have an entryway console with a drawer, measure it and determine how many categories you would like to fit within it. If you don't have a drawer, you'll create your drop zone with a labeled bin or a set of trays.

3. Place the items back in the drawer, in a bin, or on trays. With each seasonal transition, reevaluate what's in your drop zone.

4. Consider placing overstock in bins directly above the active drop zone. (For example, if you purchase small packs of tissue in bulk, place one or two down below and the rest above for a quick restock.) Seasonal items like sunscreen and bug spray can also be stored here when not in use.

MAIL

The key to keeping your mail organized is setting up a system right where you "process" it. If you don't like to open mail upon delivery, create a landing spot for it to collect. At least once a week, grab your bin and get to sorting.

1.   Designate a sensible location to keep your mail. If you don't have space in your entry, the kitchen or home office are great spots because you typically have other paperwork that needs to be processed in those areas. Once you've decided on the location, select a shelf or drawer with enough space to create a system that includes not only incoming mail but also related supplies like a mail opener and stamps.

2.   Add a paper sorter with slots for mail that needs to be filed, correspondence that requires further action (e.g., bills to pay), and items to be read on a rainy day (e.g., magazines). If you process your mail weekly rather than daily (see next step), use the leftmost slot to collect all mail until your designated processing day.

3.   Determine a schedule for when you'd like to review your mail and set calendar reminders for whoever is responsible for this task in your household.

Pro Tip

Another option is to carry your daily mail directly to your recycling bin and open it there. Simply drop junk mail and envelopes in the bin, and return the rest to your sorting system.

COATS, SHOES & ACCESSORIES

Entries are high-traffic areas of the home that require regular attention. You want to ensure that only what you currently need is within easy access, so they should be edited each season and, possibly, as hobbies transition throughout the year.

APPROX. TIME:
1 hour

ESSENTIALS:
Hangers or hooks, bins, labels, entry table or furniture with storage

EXTRAS:
Coatrack, covered rolling rack, under-bed bin, vacuum-seal bags

1. First, pull out all of your family's coats. If you have children in your home, now is a great time to check sizing and move to the next size up if necessary.

2. If you don't have a dedicated coat closet, set individual hooks or a coatrack by the door. Hang children's hooks at their height to promote independence.

3. Whether you have a dedicated coat closet or not, you should store coats only for the current season at the entry. If the closet is overstuffed, it will hamper a quick and easy exit. Off-season coats should be hung in a storage closet or bedroom closet. If you're tight on space, consider adding a covered rolling rack to your garage or folding the coats down and placing them in an under-bed bin. Puffer coats can easily be consolidated using vacuum-seal bags. Then they just need to be fluffed.

4. Next, gather everyday shoes and accessories—hats, gloves, scarves, umbrellas. Ensure that all gloves have mates and pull out anything that needs mending. These accessories can go in a bin (or multiple bins, sorted by type or household member) underneath a narrow entryway table.

→ *Accessories bins don't have to hold only hats or gloves—they should contain whatever you need when you walk out the door for your next adventure. Maybe you'll have one for blankets to take to the park or kids' on-the-go necessities like wipes, sunblock, or a prepacked tote of restaurant activities.*

Pro Tip

As with all high-traffic areas, make it a habit to do some quick upkeep on this space on a weekly basis. Perhaps time it with other Sunday tasks. It should take less than 5 minutes to ensure everything is in its place and nothing needs to be relocated.

SEASONAL TRANSITIONS

Whether you live somewhere with drastically changing seasons or not, this is still a great project for late spring and late fall. Maybe you'll be switching from hats and gloves to swim bags and sunscreen, or it may just be a matter of making sure an umbrella is within reach or the kids have the right sports equipment. Whatever the case may be, this is a moment to take stock of the organization of the entryway as a whole, to ensure that it's functioning as seamlessly as possible.

APPROX. TIME:
1 hour

EXTRAS:
Bins, labels

---

1. Touch up the entire entryway. Relocate items that don't belong and put the rest back in their designated spots.

2. Once you've tidied, evaluate whether your current system is working for everyone in the household. Can you easily find what you need when you need it? Does everything have a spot, or do you need to create space and/or add labeled bins for new categories?

3. If the system still works as is, begin removing seasonal items. This could also be a time to do shoe swaps, so that you don't forget to wear some of your favorites that have been stored away in your closet.

4. Relocate the off-season items to where they are stored in your home.

Garage

Drop Zone **188**

Home Maintenance **191**

Tools **193**

Sports & Outdoor
Activities **195**

Donations & Recycling **196**

Gardening **199**

GARAGES VARY WIDELY in terms of their size and layout, from a spacious double-story garage to a compact single-car one. Regardless of its dimensions, the key to maximizing a garage's potential lies in making the most of every inch of available space. Proper utilization of wall space and height is crucial, as garages often serve as the primary point of entry into a home, demanding both accessibility and functionality.

Whatever you're storing, avoid using cardboard boxes, which can buckle, absorb moisture, and attract pests. Opt for clearly labeled, weathertight storage bins, especially if you experience seasonal temperature changes. Solid-color bins with durable, large labels will contribute to a neater appearance.

By addressing the considerations on the opposite page and implementing a thoughtful approach to garage organization, you'll create a space that is both functional and aesthetically pleasing.

FOUR THINGS TO CONSIDER

1 **Vehicle accessibility.** Ensure that you can easily get in and out of your car without obstacles.

2 **Current usage.** Evaluate how your garage is being utilized and what other purposes you'd like it to serve. Do you have a bunch of gear for extra-curricular activities that you need to access regularly? Do you have multiple types of trimmers for your lawn? Other categories you may store here include holiday decorations, auto care products, gardening items, tools, sports/hobby equipment, beach/lake supplies, bulky kids' toys, and backstock that overflows from indoor spaces.

3 **Needed improvements.** Assess whether your space requires additional shelving or wall systems to support your organizational efforts. If so, consider the height of the space when determining the height of shelving.

4 **Seasonal transitions.** Organize items in a way that makes it simple to access in-season belongings and transition them throughout the year.

DROP ZONE

The entry from your garage to the interior of your home is a great location for a drop zone. Hopefully you also have one of these in your entryway (see page 176), but here is the place for items that may be too dirty or bulky for the interior, like shoes or in-rotation sports gear.

APPROX. TIME:
1 hour

ESSENTIALS:
Bins, labels

EXTRAS:
Shelf with hooks or small coatrack, boot tray or shelving unit

1.   First, identify the organizational furniture and accessories you'll need to establish your drop zone. Consider adding a storage shelf with hooks or a small coatrack to make use of vertical space for bags and wet coats. Small bins can be placed on the shelf for hats or outdoor items that shouldn't be applied in the home like spray sunblock or bug spray.

2.   How you organize shoes is entirely dependent on how much space you have: maybe a boot tray will have to suffice, but if you have more space, we suggest a shelving unit. (For children, sometimes a labeled shoe bin is the best way to get them to stay organized and doesn't require them to line shoes up perfectly.)

3.   Determine how much space each household member can be allotted, then edit down to current everyday items. Relocate all off-season items to bedroom closets (rain/snow boots that aren't in use should be stored elsewhere in your garage or in a coat closet).

4.   Once a week, remove items that have accumulated beyond what fits comfortably or switch some out for the season.

HOME MAINTENANCE

Within the realm of home maintenance, tasks can be categorized into two distinct types: regular and emergency maintenance. Gather your household members and engage in a collaborative effort to compile a comprehensive list of all recurring and potential emergency tasks. Ensure that you possess the necessary tools and supplies to handle each of these responsibilities at least once.

---

1.   For routine upkeep, such as changing filters or cleaning gutters, a digital calendar comes to the rescue. Even if you don't plan to tackle these tasks yourself, create calendar reminders to schedule the necessary work. If feasible, purchase enough supplies to complete these maintenance tasks at least once or twice before replenishing your stock. (In the absence of storage space, performing the task itself, such as changing a filter, can serve as a reminder to reorder for the future.)

2.   When it comes to emergency maintenance, your needs will hinge on the type of home you reside in and its geographical location. If you inhabit a single-family home in an area prone to power outages, a compact generator safely stowed in the garage might be a wise investment. In the case of plumbing woes, having essential tools like a plunger and a snake readily available can be a game changer. Be realistic about the home maintenance you will actually perform versus what you will hire a professional to do.

3.   Once you've determined what items are necessary in both everyday and emergency scenarios, you can assess how much storage space to dedicate to them. Sort the items as they would be arranged at a hardware store (e.g., plumbing, paint, HVAC, electrical).

4.   Ideally the items would be stored in the garage alongside your tools (see page 193), conveniently placed on shelves in labeled bins for quick and easy access. If you do not have available shelving, purchase a unit that will fit the space. If you do not have room for a unit, you will need to seriously consider what is essential to keep and only keep what fits your current storage.

APPROX. TIME:
1 hour

ESSENTIALS:
Bins, labels

EXTRAS:
Tool chest or toolbox,
workbench, pegboard,
shelving unit

TOOLS

Tools is a category that varies widely from household to household. Do you own or rent your home? Are you a DIYer, or is your handy-person on speed dial? The answers to these questions will determine how many items you should have on hand and how much space is actually needed.

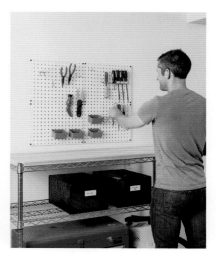

1. Gather all of your tools. Donate any duplicate items—you only need so many screwdrivers! Next, determine where these items will be stored. Do you have (or want to purchase) a tool chest with drawers or a workbench? If you are short on garage space or have an excess of tools, keep items that are most often used inside, like a tape measure or screwdriver, in a utility or laundry room.

2. In keeping with our overall garage philosophy, take advantage of vertical wall space by mounting a pegboard for hand tools. Since the space is limited, hang only the tools you reach for most often. As you determine your arrangement, group by type and consider ease of access (e.g., if you have bins for smaller items like screws, place those along the bottom so it's easier to see the contents).

3. For items that don't fit into a toolbox or on your pegboard, labeled stacking bins with lids can do the trick. Organize the items by task, such as plumbing or wall mounting, so you can take the entire bin with you if you need more than one tool. If you already have a shelving unit, first ensure that the bins you want to use will fit well on the shelves prior to sorting categories into them. If you do not already have shelving in the garage, purchase a unit that accommodates the number of bins you have.

SPORTS & OUTDOOR ACTIVITIES

Sports gear and outdoor equipment and toys often defy neat storage solutions due to their bulkiness and irregular shapes. In garages, these items can easily accumulate and turn the space into a chaotic mess. Ensuring that everyone, including children, can quickly access their gear is crucial. This is why we believe that investing in specialized storage solutions for frequently used items like skis or fishing poles is not only justified but also invaluable.

Dedicating a specific space for these items facilitates easy access and promotes an organized garage. Moreover, it encourages you to embrace your passions and hobbies, keeping them at the forefront of your lifestyle. With specialized storage, you can effortlessly grab your gear and head out to do what you love, while simultaneously maintaining a tidy, accessible garage for seamless entries and exits.

---

1. Begin by editing what you currently have. Donate any items that you no longer enjoy and any toys your children have grown out of. Toss anything that is broken or missing pieces.

2. Determine the best space and type of storage for each category. Do you need to invest in a dedicated shelving unit or any specialty solutions, such as wall hangers for kayaks or hooks for bikes or scooters? (You may need to hire a handyperson to mount wall hangers and hooks if you are not comfortable using a power drill.)

3. Organize smaller seasonal items and outdoor games in labeled bins on lower shelves near the garage door for convenient access. When they're out of season, stow these items on higher shelves.

4. Larger items will likely need to stay on the ground. Designate a parking area for kids' ride-on toys or other large items that can't be easily hung on the wall.

Pro Tip

Ensuring that children can easily reach and put away their belongings not only fosters independence but also promotes a safer and more organized environment.

DONATIONS & RECYCLING

For donations and recycling, the strategy requires a little bit of space and a lot of good habits. We like to dedicate one bin to donations and drop them off once the bin is full.

APPROX. TIME:
5 minutes

ESSENTIALS:
Bins, labels

EXTRAS:
Bags

1. Before setting an item aside for donation, ask yourself whether it is in good enough condition to give to your best friend. If it isn't, recycle it, or it will just end up in a landfill. Many cities offer textile recycling programs for clothing and/or linens that are damaged.

2. Recycling falls into two categories: everyday items and specialty items. For everyday items, use your city or county bin and position it in the garage so that it can easily be pulled out each week. Then dedicate a bin to specialty items, such as e-waste, paint, and household cleaners, and place it next to your donation bin. You may want to include smaller bags within the bin, to sort items that need to go to different drop-off sites.

Pro Tip

Create a list of the recycling centers you typically go to with their hours of operation. Either save it to your phone or tape it to the inside of the specialty recycling bin.

RECYCLING

DONATIONS

APPROX. TIME:
1 hour

ESSENTIALS:
Bins, turntable, hooks

GARDENING

A gardening station can mean anything from an actual potting bench to a simple bin holding only your essentials. As with many categories in the home, your setup will depend on the space you have and how important the category is to you. Once you've determined that, you'll know how elaborate your setup can be. Choose bins that will allow you to easily transport your necessities around the yard or garden.

When it comes to things like potting soil and fertilizer, buy only as much as will actually fit in the allotted space. Like we mentioned when discussing decanting for the kitchen (see page 49), purchase a reasonably sized container that will hold the amount of material you want to keep on hand.

1. Create a small "essentials" bin with your gloves, a small trowel, and pruning shears. If you are frequently reaching for certain tools, consider hanging them for easy access. This also allows them to dry between uses.

2. A turntable is a great option for smaller containers of plant food or root stimulator. If you have children, be sure to keep these items out of reach. Dedicate a separate bin to weed killer and fertilizer to be stored on a higher shelf when not in use.

3. Store personal accessories (like gardening shoes, sun hats, kneeling pads) in a dry location so they are ready to be used when it's time to head to the garden.

4. If you have wall space in your garage or storage area, hang larger, heavier items like shovels and rakes to prevent them from becoming tripping hazards. Just like in the bedroom (see page 76), we love hanging sun hats to keep them out of the way and to help maintain their shape.

← *If you reside in a small space and can fulfill your gardening dreams only with some indoor plants, choose a small plastic or durable bin that can be easily cleaned to store your pruning shears, plant fertilizer, potting soil, and a watering can. This bin can be kept in the garage, the kitchen, or even the laundry room.*

THE 7-DAY RESET

CONGRATULATIONS, you've organized your entire home! Now what? Welcome to NEAT's 7-Day Reset. As we've mentioned, home organization isn't one and done. Even the most fastidiously organized home will require periodic touch-ups.

When the urge to get organized strikes, it might seem like a great idea to give your space a total overhaul. But that's not always realistic. Instead of going all-in and risking burning out or running out of time before the job is completed, we have a better, more manageable suggestion: a biannual reset, requiring just 30 minutes each day for seven days. For this week, your focus will be on identifying items that don't belong in a given space, determining where they do belong, and putting systems back in place.

THE PROCESS

Spend Sunday prepping for the week. Complete the "Space" portion of the worksheet (opposite), and designate "Donate," "Recycle," and "Toss" boxes or bags. Then follow the process below as you tackle one room per day.

Sweep the entire room: Do a 5-minute sweep, identifying items that either don't belong in the space or should be removed from your home entirely.

Edit the piles: Now spend 10 minutes sorting the items from your sweep into "Relocate," "Donate," "Recycle," and "Toss" piles. Quickly relocate the items that are in the wrong space to their correct location.

Tackle the biggest pain point: Select one drawer, shelf, or bin that's been giving you problems and spend 15 minutes getting it into shape. Empty it, then sort items by type before placing each category within its own container or bin. Be strict here: you are focusing on just the *single* chosen pain point and creating a new system for it.

Reflect on the space: After you've finished the day's organizing, take a moment to fill in the "Reflection" portion of the worksheet. Are you missing something? Time to restock. Have a surplus? Stop purchasing. Need boundaries? Implement new organizational products.

THE SCHEDULE

This is a suggested schedule for your week. We chose these spaces because they are high-traffic areas that typically benefit from a reset, but your needs should determine which spaces you address—feel free to adjust the schedule accordingly.

Day 1, Sunday: Prep (see above)
Day 2, Monday: Bathroom
Day 3, Tuesday: Kitchen
Day 4, Wednesday: Pantry
Day 5, Thursday: Bedroom
Day 6, Friday: Kids' spaces or home office
Day 7, Saturday: Entryway

MONDAY	TUESDAY	WEDNESDAY
Space	Space	Space
Start Time	Start Time	Start Time
Pain Point	Pain Point	Pain Point
▨ Sweep ▨ Edit ▨ Tackle	▨ Sweep ▨ Edit ▨ Tackle	▨ Sweep ▨ Edit ▨ Tackle
Reflection	Reflection	Reflection

THURSDAY	FRIDAY	SATURDAY
Space	Space	Space
Start Time	Start Time	Start Time
Pain Point	Pain Point	Pain Point
▨ Sweep ▨ Edit ▨ Tackle	▨ Sweep ▨ Edit ▨ Tackle	▨ Sweep ▨ Edit ▨ Tackle
Reflection	Reflection	Reflection

Acknowledgments

We extend our heartfelt gratitude to our families, friends, and countless mentors whose unwavering love and support have fueled our journey. Nurturing a business and watching it flourish beyond our wildest expectations has been remarkable, made possible only by your enduring encouragement and motivation. Without you, these ambitious dreams would remain unfulfilled.

To our husbands, Mike and Alex, we offer profound gratitude for being the ultimate copilots. Your shared belief in modern-day parenting and love for this brand have transformed it into a cherished addition to our families.

To our dedicated internal team, this achievement belongs to us all. Together, we perfected the method and have now breathed life into the idea of putting it on paper to share it with the world.

Lisa Ruff, your unyielding determination, visionary concepts, and unwavering commitment to this book are the cornerstones of its existence. Our collaboration has been an extraordinary journey that means the world to us.

Lauren Combs, your creative genius is a beacon of light that illuminates every page. Your knack for visualizing and curating the perfect shot elevates our work to unparalleled heights. Thank you for sharing not only your mind but also your home as the backdrop and inspiration for these images!

We owe a special debt of gratitude to Hannah Goetz and her family for graciously opening their exquisite home to us as well. Your spaces tell the quintessential NEAT Method story, and we are deeply appreciative of your generosity.

Our heartfelt thanks extend to Martin Vecchio and his team for the beautiful imagery that graces these pages. You exude composure and professionalism on a photo shoot.

To our product development team, whose ingenuity brought our exceptional products to life, we express our sincere appreciation. The designs and their functionality are a testament to the fact that, with the right placement, any space can be transformed into an organized masterpiece.

To our franchise owners: you are the backbone of our brand. Your trust and dedication have shaped us into who we are today. Your daily inspiration propels us to strive for greatness.

To our clients: this brand would not be what it is today without those of you who have welcomed us into your private lives and trusted our teams to transform the way your homes operate. Each and every client experience has allowed us to refine and perfect our methods. We are forever grateful to those who have made this journey possible. Your trust and support have been instrumental to our growth and success.

In the vibrant landscape of the organizing community, we find ourselves among a unique and driven group of individuals. We are humbled to stand alongside fellow type A's and take pride in our collective effort to place this once-small industry firmly on the map. The journey has just begun, and there is so much more to come.

To Bridget Monroe Itkin and the rest of the Artisan family, thank you for making this dream a reality. We are forever grateful for your belief in us. Your contributions make these pages shine, and we had so much fun working alongside you!

Index

accessories
    in bedroom, 76–77
    in entryway, 180–81
art supplies, 128–29
artwork, kids', 130–31

bags
    purses and, 78–79
    reusable, 164–65
baking supplies, 48–49
"baskets" vs. "bins", 16
bathrooms and linen closets,
    86–107
    considerations for organizing,
      89
    everyday essentials, 90–91
    first aid supplies, 102–3
    guest bathroom, 104–5
    layout of, 88
    linen closet, 94–95
    makeup, 92–93
    medication, 100–101
    sheets, 96–97
    simple principles for, 88
    towels, 98–99
    travel toiletries, 106–7
bedrooms, 56–85
    closet, 80–81
    clothing storage, 60–75. *See
      also* clothing storage
    considerations for organizing,
      59
    dresser, 82–83
    jewelry and accessories, 76–77
    for kids, 108–15. *See also* kids'
      spaces
    "less is more" attitude in, 58

nightstand, 84–85
overnight guest
    accommodations, 170–71
    purses and bags, 78–79
"bins," 16, 23
books, 116–17

categorizing items, 14
cleaners, in kitchen, 52–53
closets
    bedroom, 80–81
    for kids, 112–13
    linen, 88, 94–99
clothing storage
    closets, 80–81
    coats, 180–81
    color-coding, 62, 63
    denim, 70–71
    dresser, 82–83
    file folding, 60–62
    hanging, 62–63
    kids' closet, 112–13
    kids' dress-up items, 126–27
    kids' dresser, 114–15
    setup for, 60–63
    shoes, 74–75
    sweaters, 66–67
    T-shirts, 64–65
    undergarments, 72–73
    workout apparel, 68–69
coats, 180–81
color-coding clothing, 62, 63
containers
    "bins," 16, 23
    food storage, 36–37
    for organizing, 16, 23
cooking tools, 32–33

cookware, 30–31
cosmetics, 92–93

decanting products, 16, 19
deciding what goes where, 15
denim, 70–71
detergents, laundry, 138–39
dish towels, 28–29
donations, 196–97
dress-up items, 126–27
dressers
    adult, 82–83
    kids', 114–15
drop zones
    in entryway, 176–77
    in or near garage, 188–89

editing step, 15
entertaining supplies, 158–59
entryway, 172–83
    coats, shoes, and accessories,
      180–81
    considerations for organizing,
      175
    drop zone, 176–77
    mail, 178–79
    seasonal transitions, 182–83
everyday essentials
    in bathroom, 90–91
    in kitchen for morning routine,
      50–51

file folding, 60–62
first aid supplies, 102–3
folding
    denim, 70–71
    file folding, 60–62

folding *(cont.)*
sheets, 96
sweaters, 66–67
T-shirts, 64–65
towels, 98
food storage containers, 36–37

garage, 184–99
considerations for organizing,
187
donations and recycling,
196–97
drop zone, 188–89
gardening, 198–99
home maintenance, 190–91
sports and outdoor activities,
194–95
tools, 192–93
gardening supplies and
equipment, 198–99
gift wrap, 162–63
guests
bathroom for, 104–5
overnight accommodations
for, 170–71

hanging clothing, 62–63
hobbies, 160–61
holiday decor, 168–69
home maintenance equipment,
190–91
home office, 148–49
homework station, 132–33

jeans, 70–71
jewelry, 76–77

keepsakes, 150–51
kids' artwork, 130–31
kids' spaces, 108–33
art supplies, 128–29
books, 116–17
closet, 112–13

considerations for organizing,
111
dress-up, 126–27
dresser, 114–15
homework station, 132–33
kids' artwork, 130–31
Legos, 124–25
playroom, 122–23
stuffed animals, 118–19
"treasures," 120–21
kids' tableware, 38–39
kitchen and pantry, 24–55
baking supplies, 48–49
cleaners and under-sink
supplies, 52–53
cooking tools, 32–33
cookware, 30–31
dish towels, 28–29
food storage containers,
36–37
kids' tableware, 38–39
layout of, 26–27
morning routine items,
50–51
multipurpose drawer, 54–55
pantry, 27, 44–45
refrigerator, 42–43
snacks, 46–47
spices, 34–35
water bottles, 40–41

labeling, 18–19
laundry, 134–43
considerations for organizing,
137
detergents and laundry tools,
138–39
laundry systems, 140–41
lost and found, 142–43
layout
of bathroom, 88
of kitchen and pantry, 26–27
Legos, 124–25

linen closets, 88, 94–99. *See also*
bathrooms and linen closets
considerations for organizing,
89
sheets, 96–97
towels, 98–99
lost and found, 142–43
luggage, 166–67

mail, 178–79
maintaining organization, 20
maintenance equipment,
190–91
makeup, 92–93
measurements, recording, 17
medication, 100–101
morning routine items
everyday essentials in
bathroom, 90–91
in kitchen, 50–51
multipurpose drawer, in kitchen,
54–55

NEAT Method, 9–10, 14–23
adding organizational products
step in, 16–17
deciding what goes where step
in, 15
editing step in, 15
maintaining step in, 20
organizing kit for, 22–23
putting it all together step in,
19
7-Day Reset, 201–3
sorting and categorizing step
in, 14
nightstands, 84–85

office, home, 148–49
organization
as a habit, 13
NEAT Method for (*See* NEAT
Method)

organizational products
    labeling, 18–19
    organizing kit, 22–23
    selecting, 16–17
outdoor equipment and toys, 194–95
overnight guest accommodations, 170–71

pantry, 27, 44–45. *See also* kitchen and pantry
paperwork, 148–49
personal technology, 152–53
pet supplies, 154–55
playroom, 122–23
pots and pans, 30–31
purses, 78–79

recycling, 196–97
refrigerator, 42–43
reusable bags, 164–65

seasonal items, in entryway, 182–83
7-Day Reset, 201–3
sheets, 96–97
shoes
    in bedroom, 74–75
    in entryway, 180–81
snacks, 46–47

sorting items, 14
spices, 34–35
sports gear, 194–95
storage and utility spaces, 144–71
    considerations for organizing, 147
    entertaining supplies, 158–59
    gift wrap, 162–63
    hobbies, 160–61
    holiday decor, 168–69
    home office and paperwork, 148–49
    keepsakes, 150–51
    luggage and travel gear, 166–67
    overnight guest accommodations, 170–71
    personal technology, 152–53
    pet supplies, 154–55
    reusable bags, 164–65
    utility items, 156–57
stuffed animals, 118–19
sweaters, 66–67

T-shirts, 64–65
tableware, kids', 38–39
technology, personal, 152–53
toiletries
    everyday essentials, 90–91
    travel, 106–7

tools
    cooking, 32–33
    in garage, 192–93
    for home maintenance, 190–91
tote bags, 164–65
towels
    bathroom, 98–99
    dish towels, 28–29
toys
    Legos, 124–25
    outdoor, 194–95
    playroom, 122–23
travel gear, 166–67
travel toiletries, 106–7
"treasures," kids', 120–21

under-sink spaces
    kitchen supplies in, 52–53
    measuring, 17
undergarments, 72–73
utility items, 156–57.
    See also storage and utility spaces

water bottles, 40–41
workout apparel, 68–69

zones, 15

ASHLEY MURPHY AND MARISSA HAGMEYER are the founders of NEAT Method, a luxury home organizing brand with a hundred franchises across North America and an exclusive line of organizing products that can be found at retailers such as Crate & Barrel, Food52, and Saks Fifth Avenue. Murphy and Hagmeyer have been featured in countless media outlets including the *New York Times*, *Vogue*, *Good Morning America*, *Today*, *Real Simple*, and Apartment Therapy.